SINGER

SEWING REFERENCE LIBRARY®

Sewing Lingerie

Cy DeCosse Incorporated
Minnetonka, Minnesota

SINGER

SEWING REFERENCE LIBRARY®

Sewing Lingerie

Contents

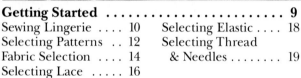

Copyright © 1991
Cy DeCosse Incorporated
5900 Green Oak Drive
Minnetonka, Minnesota 55343
1-800-328-3895
All rights reserved
Printed in U.S.A.

Also available from the publisher:
*Sewing Essentials, Sewing for the Home,
Clothing Care & Repair, Sewing for Style,
Sewing Specialty Fabrics, Sewing
Activewear, The Perfect Fit, Timesaving
Sewing, More Sewing for the Home,
Tailoring, Sewing for Children, Sewing
with an Overlock, 101 Sewing Secrets,
Sewing Pants That Fit, Quilting by
Machine, Decorative Machine Stitching,
Creative Sewing Ideas*

Library of Congress
Cataloging-in-Publication Data

Sewing Lingerie

p. cm. — (Singer sewing reference
library)
Includes index.
ISBN 0-86573-260-4
ISBN 0-86573-261-2 (pbk.)
1. Lingerie. 2. Sewing. I. Series.
TT670.S49 1991
646.4'204 — dc20   90-21094

Distributed by: Contemporary Books, Inc.
  Chicago, Illinois

CY DECOSSE INCORPORATED
Chairman: Cy DeCosse
President: James B. Maus
Executive Vice President: William B. Jones

SEWING LINGERIE
Created by: The Editors of Cy DeCosse
Incorporated, in cooperation with the
Sewing Education Department, Singer
Sewing Company. Singer is a trademark
of The Singer Company and is used
under license.

Executive Editor: Zoe A. Graul
Technical Director: Rita C. Opseth
Project Manager: Linda Halls
Senior Art Director: Lisa Rosenthal
Writer: Rita C. Opseth
Editors: Janice Cauley, Bernice Maehren
Sample Coordinator: Carol Olson
Technical Photo Director: Bridget Haugh
Fabric Editor: Joanne Wawra
Sewing Staff: Phyllis Galbraith, Bridget
  Haugh, Sara Holmen, Linda Neubauer,
  Carol Olson, Lori Ritter, Nancy
  Sundeen, Barbara Vik
*Director of Development, Planning
  & Production:* Jim Bindas
Photo Studio Manager: Rebecca DaWald

Photographers: Rex Irmen, John Lauenstein,
  Bill Lindner, Mark Macemon,
  Charles Nields, Mette Nielsen, Mike
  Parker, Cathleen Shannon
Production Manager: Amelia Merz
Electronic Publishing Analyst:
  Kevin D. Frakes
Production Staff: Janice Cauley, Joe
  Fahey, Melissa Grabanski, Jim Huntley,
  Mark Jacobson, Duane John, Yelena
  Konrardy, Daniel Meyers, Linda
  Schloegel, Greg Wallace, Nik Wogstad
Consultants: Ronda Chaney, Kathryn M.
  Johnson, Andrea Nynas, Nancy Palma
Contributors: And Sew On; Burda Patterns,
  Inc.; Butterick Patterns; Dell Fabrics;

Exotic Silks; Land o' Lace; The McCall
Pattern Company; Minnetonka Mills,
Inc.; Pellon Division, Freudenberg
Nonwovens; Rhode Island Textile
Company; Simplicity Pattern Co. Inc.;
Stretch & Sew, Inc.; Treadle Yard
Goods; Vogue Patterns
Color Separations: Scantrans Pte. Ltd.
Printing: Ringier America, Inc. (0391)

Introduction

Lingerie, including intimate apparel, loungewear, and sleepwear, is fun to sew. Working with lovely laces and fine fabrics is very rewarding, and the sewing techniques shown in this book are streamlined for easier construction. Whether you want to sew a simple sleep shirt or an elegant camisole, patterns are available from many different pattern companies. You can make lingerie from easy-care knits, such as tricots and single knits, or from luxurious silky wovens, including charmeuse.

The Getting Started section of the book will guide you in all your choices, from the right pattern size to the most appropriate lingerie fabrics and laces. There is also a chart to help you choose which elastic to use and what length to cut it for each project you sew.

The Basic Sewing Techniques section offers helpful advice for cutting slippery lingerie fabrics and then takes you through the basic steps of flat and in-the-round construction. Directions for appropriate seam finishes and edge finishes are given, as well as several methods for applying lace and elastic. For example, choose a delicately scalloped picot edge finish for the lower edge of a slip, or for a different look, apply an intricately detailed lace. Conceal elastic by encasing it with fabric, or use an exposed method to apply a decorative elastic, such as picot-edged lingerie elastic or stretch lace.

In the Intimate Apparel section, you will learn how to sew basic lingerie, including half slips, full slips, camisoles, and panties. Specialty garments, such as French bikinis, tap pants, teddies, sports bras, and leggings, are also included. In addition to step-by-step sewing instructions, you will also be shown creative ways to vary a look with embellishments.

The Loungewear and Sleepwear section offers many innovative techniques for sewing simple sleep shirts and pajamas as well as ruffled nightgowns. Discover the secret for pucker-free fine piping on silky sleep shirts, and learn a simple way to sew the fly front on boxer shorts. Follow the easy steps to make a warm terry-lined robe or a kimono that is perfect for lounging.

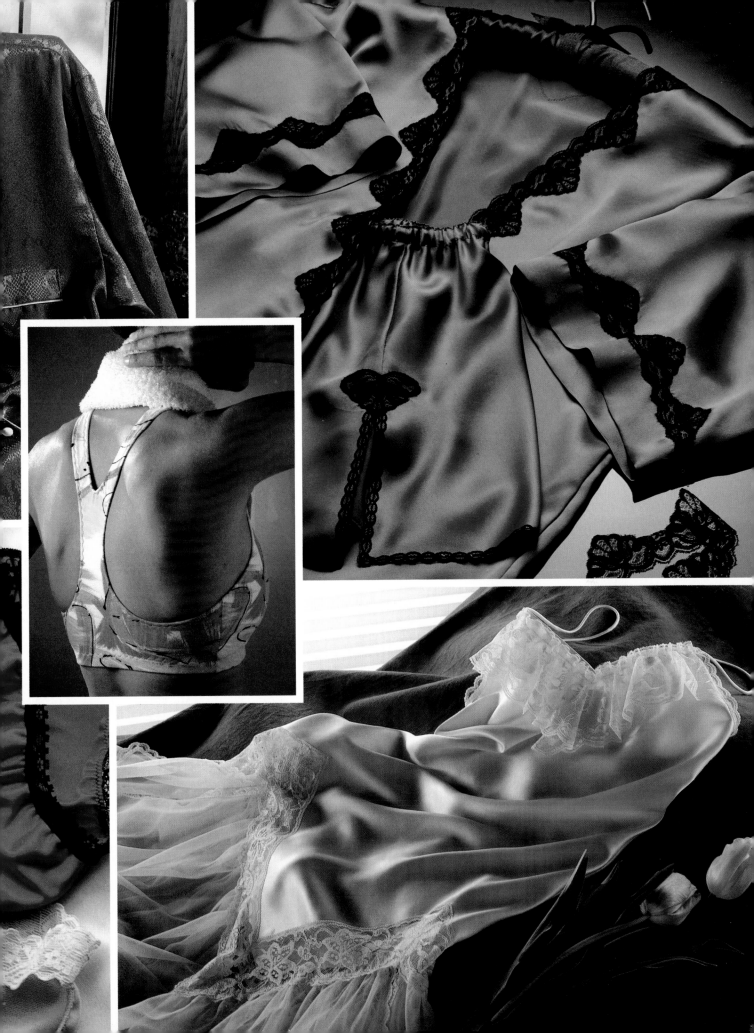

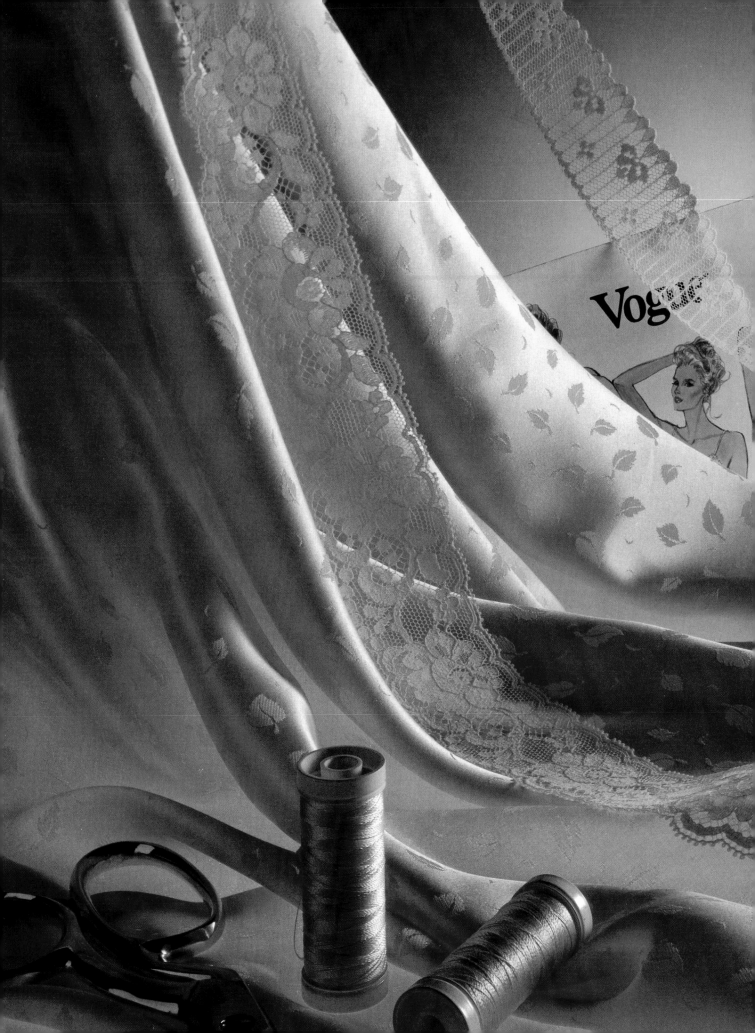

Sewing Lingerie

Lingerie can be sewn quickly and easily, often at a fraction of the cost of ready-to-wear. The wide variety of beautiful laces and fine fabrics available in fabric stores makes lingerie sewing even more rewarding.

Lingerie is divided into two main categories: intimate apparel and loungewear. Intimate apparel, sometimes called daywear, includes the garments that are worn under street clothing, such as slips, panties, tap pants, and teddies. Use silky fabrics or fine batistes for luxurious intimate apparel. Or use cotton interlocks and pointelles for panties and camisoles.

Loungewear includes garments worn for lounging at home or for sleeping. You can sew silky boxers for men or elegant lacy peignoirs for women. Pajamas, robes, and kimonos are popular items to sew for both men and women.

One of the advantages in sewing lingerie is getting the fit you want. Lingerie should have some ease so it does not pull or bind, but not enough to cause excess bulk. For a smooth fit under street clothes, a camisole or full slip should skim the body at the bustline, with no gaping at the upper edge. Lingerie made from knits or bias-cut wovens can be fitted more closely to the body than garments from woven fabrics cut on the straight of grain. With knits and bias-cut wovens, a smooth fit is achieved over the bustline if the garment measures the same as, or slightly smaller than, the full bust measurement; at the hipline, 2" (5 cm) of ease is adequate.

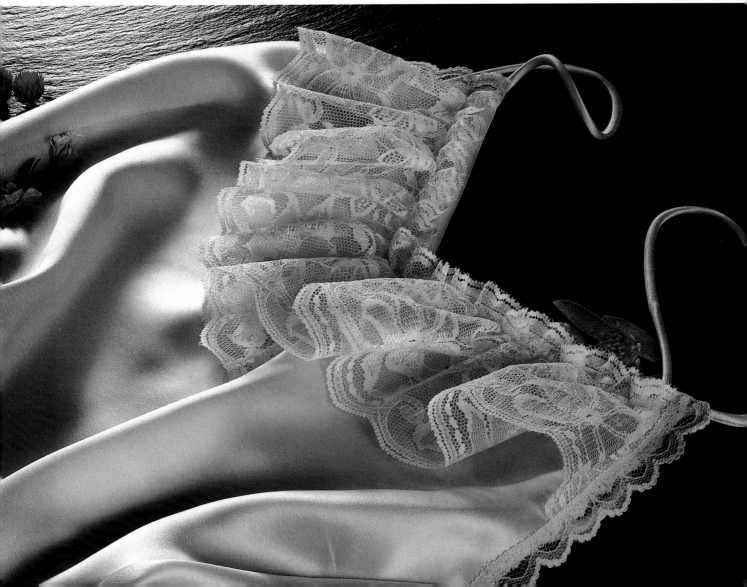

Selecting Patterns

Lingerie patterns, in a variety of styles, are available from several pattern companies. Some patterns are designed to be used for knits only; others may be designed for woven fabrics. Keep in mind that a pattern designed for knits or bias-cut wovens will have less ease or fullness than a pattern designed for woven fabrics cut on the straight of grain.

You will notice some differences in patterns; for example, some allow 5/8" (1.5 cm) seam allowances, while others allow 1/4" or 3/8" (6 mm or 1 cm). Also the amount of ease allowed may vary from one pattern to another.

Select a camisole, full slip, or teddy pattern based on your full bust measurement if you wear a bra with a B-cup or smaller; select the pattern based on your high bust measurement if you wear a bra with a

C-cup or larger. Select a half slip or pantie pattern by your hip measurement. If you require one pattern size at the bustline and another at the hipline, you may want to select a multisize pattern.

A few pattern adjustments may be necessary in order to achieve good fit, especially in full slips, camisoles, and teddies. Directions for adjusting the pattern are included in each garment section.

Using the instructions in this book, you can change some of the techniques that are given in the pattern directions. This will allow you to vary the look of the garments or to use different types of elastics. When you plan to use a different technique, keep in mind that seam or hem allowances may need to be changed when you lay out the pattern.

Taking Measurements

The first step toward achieving good fit is to take correct body measurements. These will be used to select the correct pattern size and to determine whether any pattern adjustments will be necessary.

Measurements should be taken over a properly fitted bra; it may be helpful to be fitted for a bra by a professional to ensure a good fit.

High bust. Hold tape measure under arms and measure straight across the back, angling the tape measure in front.

Full bust. Measure over fullest part of bust and straight across back, keeping tape measure straight.

Waist. Tie narrow elastic or string at waist to determine the natural waistline. Measure body at location marked by elastic.

Bust point to waist. Measure from bust point to elastic at natural waistline, holding tape measure straight. This measurement is necessary only if your bra cup size is larger than a B-cup.

Hipline. Measure body at fullest part of the hips, as viewed from the side.

Back waist length. Measure from center of prominent bone at neck to elastic at waist.

Crotch length. Measure from the waistline at center back, between legs, to waistline at center front, holding tape measure snug against the body.

Hip depth. Measure from waistline to hipline at side.

Side length. Measure from waistline to desired length of garment.

Fabric Selection

Several luxurious fabrics are available for sewing lingerie. Lightweight, easy-care fabrics of cotton, silk, or synthetic fiber content, in either knits or wovens, may be used.

Fabrics of 100 percent cotton are durable and machine washable. Because cotton is a natural fiber, it is absorbent and breathes well, making it comfortable to wear. Cotton single knits and lightweight batistes are the most popular cotton lingerie fabrics.

Silk is a smooth and luxurious fabric. Like cotton, silk is a natural fiber that is absorbent and breathes well. Many silks are machine washable.

Nylon and polyester are the most commonly used synthetics for lingerie. They are smooth, wrinkle-resistant, durable, and machine washable. Nylon tricot and polyester charmeuse are frequently used.

If you plan to wear the lingerie under a sheer garment, you may want to choose a flesh-colored fabric to eliminate show-through.

Fabrics should be prewashed to help prevent skipped stitches and to preshrink them. When prewashing fabric, use the same fabric care method you intend to use for the finished garment.

Warm loungewear fabrics (left to right) include brushed nylon, cotton flannel, flannel-backed satin, and terry cloth.

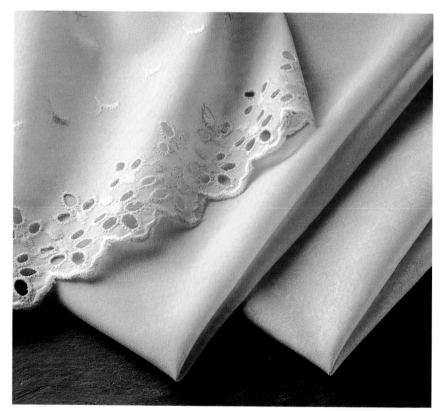

Crisp woven fabrics (left to right) used for lingerie include eyelets and lightweight plain and printed batistes, of 100 percent cotton or of a cotton/polyester blend.

Tricot does not run or ravel. It may have either a satiny sheen (left) or a matte finish (middle), and is available in several weights, including sheers (right). The widths of tricot range from 54" to 108" (137 to 274.5 cm).

Knit fabrics include cotton pointelles (left), which are knitted in various designs; pointelles may be used as an alternative to single knits. Spandex is added to some knit fabrics for greater stretch and recovery; decorative allover stretch laces (middle), as well as plain-knit spandex fabrics (right), are available.

Silky woven fabrics include silk or polyester jacquard (left) and charmeuse (right). Jacquards, with various woven-in designs, have sheen; some are soft and supple, while others have more body. Charmeuse is a high-luster, supple fabric that is especially luxurious.

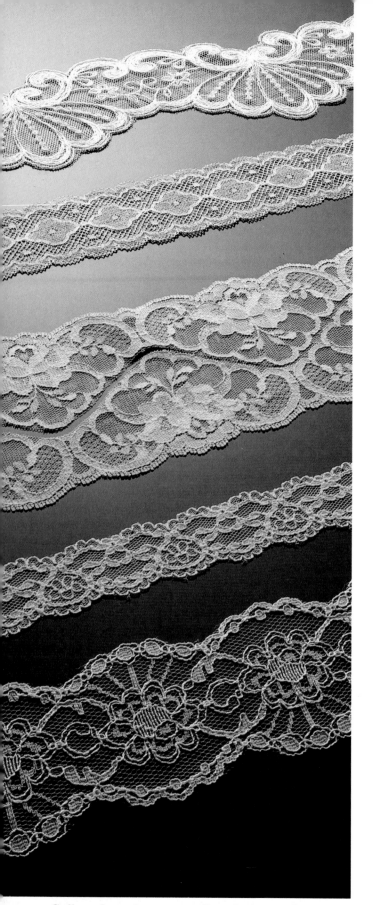

Appliqués are lace motifs that may either be purchased or cut from lace fabric.

Selecting Lace

Lace adds a feminine touch to lingerie and is frequently used as an edge finish or insert. Select lace according to the type of fabric in the garment and the placement of the lace.

Nylon lace may be used for all types of fabric, but is especially recommended for synthetic fabrics, such as nylon and polyester. It is not necessary to preshrink nylon lace.

Fine cotton laces, such as those used in French machine sewing, are softer and more comfortable next to the skin and are recommended for use with cotton and silk fabrics. Cotton eyelet, which is a heavier lace, may also be used with cotton fabric. All cotton laces should be preshrunk by pressing them thoroughly with a steam iron.

Laces have definite right and wrong sides. The right side of lace frequently has detailing that is raised, such as *cordonnets,* or cords. On the wrong side, laces often have a less finished appearance.

Galloon laces have two scalloped edges and are frequently used as borders at hemlines. Some galloon laces can be cut in half lengthwise, following the shape of the motifs, to create a narrower lace.

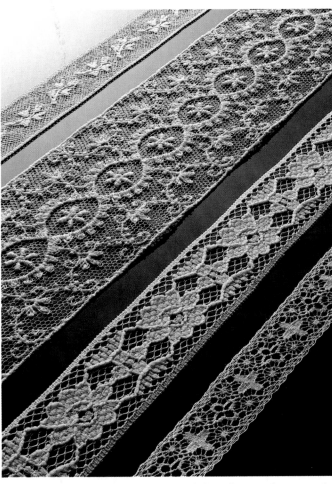

Insertion laces have two straight edges and are used as inserts or band trims.

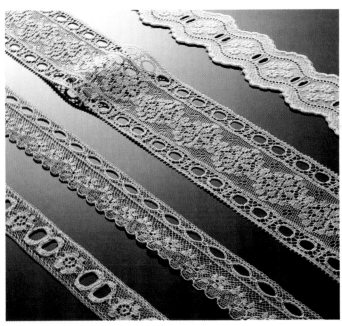

Beading laces have openings for threading ribbon. Beading may be an edging, insertion, or galloon lace.

Edgings have one straight and one scalloped edge. The straight edge is stitched to the garment, and the scalloped edge is positioned at the outer edge.

17

Selecting Elastic

Choose elastic that is lightweight, to avoid unnecessary bulk. The cut length is determined by the type of elastic and where it will be used. The pattern you select will specify a certain type and the cut length. If you want to substitute a different type of elastic, either use the guidelines in the chart below or cut the elastic for a comfortable fit, opposite.

Lingerie elastic (**a**) usually has one picot edge and one straight edge. It is softer and more comfortable than regular elastic. Use a ½" (1.3 cm) width at waistlines and a ¼" (6 mm) width at leg openings.

Plush lingerie elastic (**b**), which is felt-backed, is especially comfortable next to the skin.

Stretch lace (**c**), also designed specifically for sewing lingerie, is available in several widths. Use a 1" to 2" (2.5 to 5 cm) width at waistlines and a ½" (1.3 cm) width at leg openings.

Regular elastic (**d**) may be substituted for lingerie elastic. Cotton swimwear elastic is recommended, because of its excellent stretch and recovery. For half slips and panties, ⅜" (1 cm) cotton swimwear elastic is usually used at waistlines and ¼" (6 mm) elastic is used at leg openings. For pajamas and boxer shorts, wider regular elastic is used.

Baby elastic (**e**) may be used at the waistline of a teddy, camisole, or gown to keep the garment from shifting at the waistline.

Brief elastic (**f**) is a decorative elastic frequently used for cotton panties and sports bras. It is usually 1" to 2" (2.5 to 5 cm) wide.

Transparent elastic (**g**) is lightweight and may be used for bindings at pantie legs or at waistline seams of teddies, camisoles, and nightgowns.

Guidelines For Selecting Elastic

Type of Elastic	Width	Cut Length	Application Method
Lingerie elastic and plush lingerie elastic Used for half slips and panties	½" (1.3 cm) for waistlines; ¼" (6 mm) for leg openings	4" to 6" (10 to 15 cm) less than body measurement for waistlines and standard leg openings; three-fourths of garment opening for high-cut leg openings	Reinforced (page 56) Overlock (page 57) Overlap (page 57)
Stretch lace Used for half slips, panties, sleep bras, and negligees	½" to 2" (1.3 to 5 cm) for waistlines; ½" (1.3 cm) for leg openings and necklines	three-fourths of garment opening; for natural waistline, measure for elastic, opposite	Overlap (page 57)
Regular elastic Used for half slips, panties, pajamas, boxer shorts, and sports bras	¼" to ⅜" (6 mm to 1 cm) for waistlines of half slips and panties; ¼" (6 mm) for leg openings of panties; 1" to 2" (2.5 to 5 cm) for pajamas, boxer shorts, and sports bras	4" (10 cm) less than body measurement for waistlines and standard leg openings; three-fourths of garment opening for high-cut leg openings	Covered (page 58) Casing (page 58) Binding (page 59)
Baby elastic Used for waistlines of teddies, camisoles, and gowns	⅛" (3 mm)	4" to 6" (10 to 15 cm) less than body measurement	Elasticized Waistline (page 94)
Brief elastic Used for cotton panties and sports bras	1¹⁄₁₆" to 2¼" (2.7 to 6 cm)	4" (10 cm) less than garment opening for low-cut panties; 1" (2.5 cm) less than garment opening for sports bras	Overlap (page 57)
Transparent elastic Used for bindings on pantie legs and waistlines of teddies, camisoles, and gowns	¼" to ⅜" (6 mm to 1 cm)	4" to 6" (10 to 15 cm) less than body measurement	Binding (page 59) Elasticized Waistline (page 94)

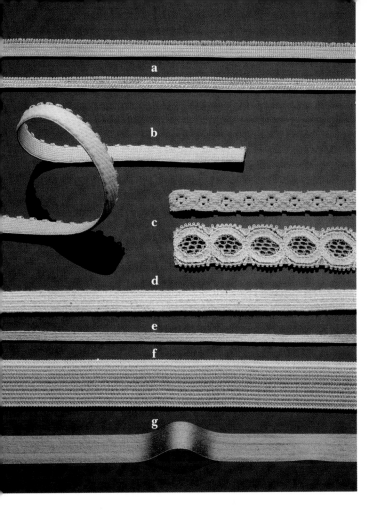

a

b

c

d

e

f

g

How to Measure for Elastic

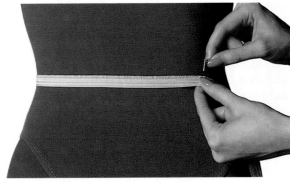

1) **Place** elastic around body at correct wearing position, snugging it to a comfortable fit; pin.

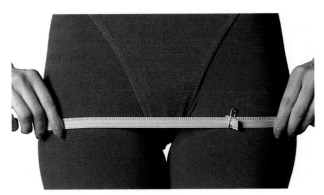

2) **Check** the fit of waistline elastic over hip area to ensure that elastic stretches adequately.

Selecting Thread & Needles

Use a fine, lightweight thread and a small needle size for sewing lingerie fabric to prevent the fabric from puckering and to prevent skipped stitches.

The fiber content of the thread should be compatible with the fiber content of the fabric. Long-staple polyester thread is recommended for sewing synthetic fabrics, such as those of polyester and nylon. Lightweight cotton thread, such as fine machine embroidery thread, is recommended for sewing fine fabrics of natural fibers, such as cotton batiste and silk charmeuse. Lightweight cotton-wrapped polyester thread is a good choice for sewing lingerie fabric of any fiber content.

Rayon thread, which has a subtle sheen, may be used for embellishments on lingerie, such as decorative machine stitching and monograms.

The size and type of needle is important, whether you are sewing with a conventional or an overlock sewing machine. For either machine, use a size 70/9 or 80/11 needle for sewing lightweight lingerie fabrics. For sewing heavier loungewear fabrics, such as terry cloth, a size 90/14 needle is used. Change the needle frequently. Even needles that are only slightly damaged or dull can cause skipped stitches or snagged fabrics.

For conventional machines, ballpoint needles are recommended for sewing knit lingerie fabrics, such as tricot and cotton knit, and for elastics. Sharps are used for sewing woven lingerie fabrics, including cottons and silks. Universal needles may be used for sewing all types of fabrics and elastics.

When using an overlock machine, special overlock needles may be required, depending on the brand and model of the machine. Refer to the manual for your machine. If your overlock machine uses standard needles, select ballpoints, universals, or sharps as for conventional sewing machines.

Basic Sewing Techniques

Laying Out & Cutting the Pattern

Before laying out the pattern, decide which methods you will use for applying elastic, sewing seams and hems, or finishing edges. If they are different from those recommended for the pattern, it may be necessary to adjust the seam or hem allowances of the pattern. The instructions for the techniques in this book give the seam or hem allowances required.

When using tricot, jersey, and single-knit fabrics, lay the pattern pieces on the lengthwise grain, which runs along the ribs in the knit; the crosswise grain, with the greatest amount of stretch, will go around the body when the garment is worn. Place all pattern pieces in the same direction. A slip is less likely to ride up or cling if you position the pattern pieces so the loops of the knit are down; determine the direction of the loops by examining the fabric with a magnifying glass.

To identify the right side of a knit fabric, stretch the fabric on the crosswise grain; the fabric will curl to the right side. Mark the wrong side of each garment section with a piece of transparent tape before removing the pattern.

When woven fabrics are used, the garment sections are often cut on the bias so the garment will drape softly. The bias cut will also provide some stretch for a better fit. Some patterns are specifically designed for a bias cut; if they are not, the grainline of the pattern may be changed.

When laying out the pattern on slippery fabrics or on the bias, it is easier and more accurate to use full-size pattern pieces and cut a single layer of fabric.

For accurate cutting, lingerie fabrics should be cut using sharp shears or a rotary cutter with a new, sharp blade. Use fine pins to prevent snagging the fabric, or use pattern weights instead of pins to hold the fabric in place during cutting. Do not allow the fabric to hang over the edge of the table; the fabric may stretch out of shape.

Tips for Positioning the Pattern on a Knit Fabric

Use with-nap layout for knit fabrics. Examine fabric, using a magnifying glass, and position pattern pieces on fabric so loops of knit are down. This helps prevent slips from riding up or clinging.

Identify direction of grainline and right side of knit fabric. Crosswise grain has greatest amount of stretch; lay out pattern pieces so crosswise grain goes around body. Fabric curls to right side when it is stretched on crosswise grain.

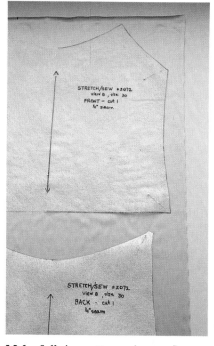

Make full-size pattern pieces; place on single layer of fabric, right sides up, with pattern grainline on the lengthwise grain of the fabric.

22

How to Position the Pattern on the Bias of a Woven Fabric

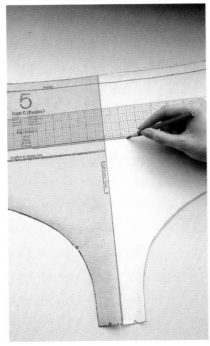

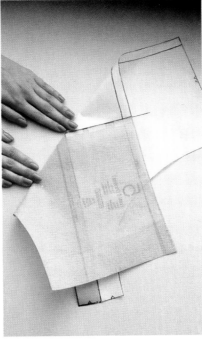

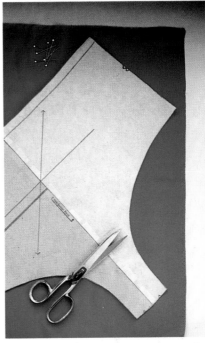

1) Make full-size pattern pieces. Mark a line at right angle to the grainline, across pattern piece.

2) Fold pattern, matching marked line and grainline. Mark a new grainline along fold.

3) Place pattern on single layer of fabric, right sides up, with the new grainline on lengthwise grain of fabric. Cut fabric.

Two Ways to Cut Lingerie Fabrics

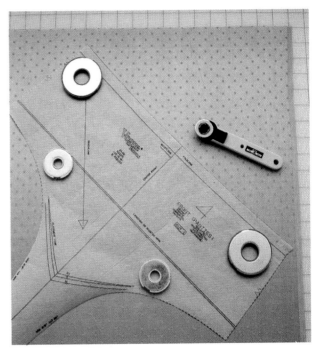

Push pins straight down through the pattern seam allowance, fabric, and cardboard or padded surface to secure slippery fabric; cut, using sharp shears. Label wrong side of fabric, using piece of transparent tape.

Place fabric on cutting mat, and use pattern weights instead of pins. Cut fabric, using rotary cutter with a new blade; hold pattern in place with hand, and apply steady, firm pressure on blade. Label wrong side of fabric, using piece of transparent tape.

Sewing Seams

Lingerie seams must be durable, to withstand repeated launderings, yet narrow, to minimize bulk. There are several methods for stitching the seams, using either the conventional or the overlock machine. Depending on the technique used, it may be necessary to adjust the seam allowances when cutting the fabric. The seam allowances on patterns vary from 1/4" to 5/8" (6 mm to 1.5 cm).

When sewing slippery lingerie fabrics, carefully pin the seam allowances together to prevent the layers from shifting as you sew. When starting to stitch the seam, hold the thread tails in one hand to encourage the fabric to feed evenly without jamming.

It is generally advisable to use directional sewing for lightweight lingerie fabrics, stitching all seams in the same direction. This ensures that all seams stretch the same way. When sewing tricots, stitch all seams against the grain, or from top to bottom, to prevent the fabric from stretching out of shape at the seamline.

Narrow French seams are used for a quality finish on woven fabrics, such as batiste or silk charmeuse, that have been cut on the straight of grain. Allow 5/8" (1.5 cm) seam allowances when cutting out the fabric.

Conventionally stitched seams may be used on all fabric types and are especially appropriate for sewing tricots and bias-cut wovens. Stretch the fabric as you stitch, for smooth, unpuckered seams that have the same amount of stretch as the fabric. Seams may be stitched using any width seam allowance, but they are trimmed to 1/4" (6 mm) after they are finished, to reduce bulk. The seam allowances may appear narrower while the seam is being stretched and stitched, especially if the seam is on the bias. Generally, a 5/8" (1.5 cm) bias seam allowance narrows to 1/2" (1.3 cm) when stretched, but a 1/4" (6 mm) seam allowance narrows very little. You may want to sew a test seam to determine how far from the raw edge you should stitch.

The balanced 3-thread overlock stitch is especially suitable for knits, but may also be used for seams in woven fabrics, provided the seam will not be subjected to a great deal of stress.

The flatlock stitch, sewn on an overlock machine, or serger, is less bulky than the 3-thread overlock stitch and is used only for knits.

When you sew the seams on an overlock machine, it is not necessary to adjust the width of the seam allowances when cutting out the fabric; the seam allowances are trimmed by the overlock knives as you sew.

How to Pin-baste Slippery Fabrics

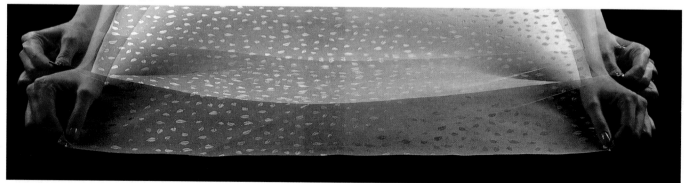

1) Place garment sections, right sides together and raw edges even, on flat surface; pin together at ends. Hold ends, and lift fabric from table. Lay fabric down again, allowing it to fall naturally into place.

Seams: (left to right) narrow French, conventionally stitched, balanced 3-thread overlock, flatlock.

2) Match raw edges, and pin layers together at center of seam, then along edge.

How to Sew a Narrow French Seam

1) Cut garment sections, allowing ⅝" (1.5 cm) seam allowances. Stitch seam, wrong sides together, ½" (1.3 cm) from edge, using about 14 stitches per inch (2.5 cm). Press seam flat on both sides.

2) Press seam open; use point presser, if desired. Then press seam closed, right sides together.

3) Trim seam allowances as close to stitching as possible, using sharp shears.

4) Pin seam, right sides together, placing one pin at each end of seam, then placing pins along seamline. Stitch ⅛" (3 mm) from fold, enclosing raw edges. Press seam allowances to one side.

How to Sew a Conventionally Stitched Seam

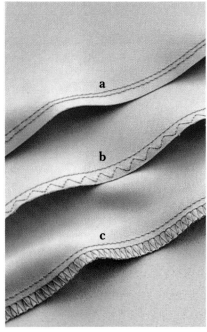

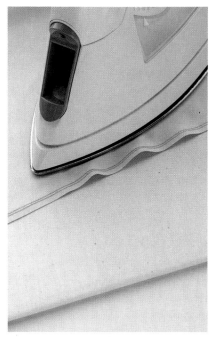

1) Stitch seam, using 12 to 15 stitches per inch (2.5 cm), stretching fabric slightly as you sew. Seam allowances may appear narrower when they are stretched; adjust distance from the raw edge to the stitching line, as necessary (page 24).

2) Finish seam by stitching within seam allowance next to first row of stitching, using straight stitch, as in step 1 **(a)**, or using 3-step zigzag stitch **(b)**; trim seam allowance close to stitching. Or use overlock stitch, trimming the excess seam allowance with knives **(c)**.

3) Press seam flat, with right sides together. If seam is distorted, reshape fabric while pressing. Press seam allowances to one side.

How to Sew a 3-thread Overlock Seam

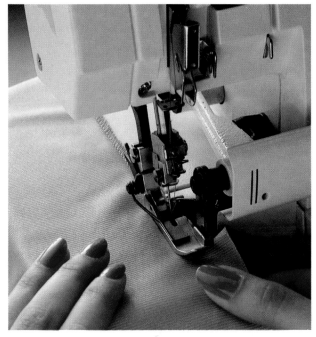

Stitch seam, right sides together, using balanced 3-thread overlock stitch on overlock machine.

How to Sew a Flatlock Seam

Stitch seam with matching thread, right sides together, using 3-thread flatlock tension on overlock machine. Pull crosswise on seam, pulling stitches flat; ladder of stitches will show on right side.

Edge Finishes

An edge finish can add a decorative effect to lingerie or simply finish off the edge. Edge finishes are usually substituted for facings, which may not stay smoothly in place. An edge finish should stabilize the edge of the lingerie without adding unnecessary bulk.

Edgestitched finishes (top, right) are neat, nonbulky finishes for woven fabrics.

Bound edge finishes (middle, right) stabilize the edge with a matching or contrasting trim. Bound edges are suitable for both wovens and knits.

Lace-trimmed bound edges (bottom, right) have a concealed binding that encases the raw edge. This finish is frequently used for lightweight cotton fabrics.

Picot edge finishes (below), used for knits, add a scalloped edging to lingerie. They can be sewn with or without a contrasting trim.

Picot Edge Finishes

The picot edge finish is a delicately scalloped edging for knit fabrics and is achieved by using the blindstitch, overedge stitch, or blanket stitch. The picot edge finish with an added contrasting trim gives extra stability to the edge of the garment.

Use lightweight fabrics, such as tricot and single knits; select those with good recovery for best results.

Allow ⅜" (1 cm) seam or hem allowances on the edges that will be finished with picot edge finishes.

How to Sew a Picot Edge Finish

1) Press ⅜" (1 cm) seam allowance or hem allowance to wrong side of fabric.

2a) Set machine for wide, long overedge stitch or blanket stitch. Stitch so right swing of needle stitches over folded edge and remaining stitches are on fabric.

How to Sew a Picot Edge Finish with Contrasting Trim

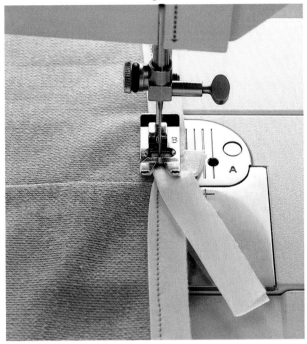

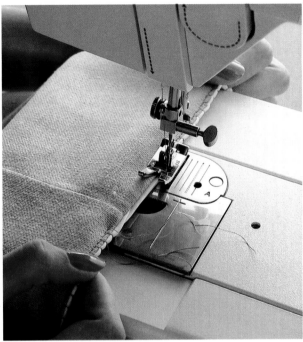

1) Cut strip of knit fabric on crosswise grain, 1⅛" (2.7 cm) wide by the length of edge plus 1" to 2" (2.5 to 5 cm). Fold strip in half lengthwise, wrong sides together. Place on right side of fabric, matching raw edges. Stitch ⅜" (1 cm) seam; overlap ends of binding, and curve ends into seam allowance.

2) Fold strip to wrong side. Stitch as in step 2a or 2b, below. Trim fabric from wrong side, close to stitching.

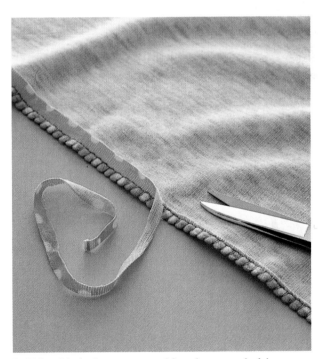

2b) Set machine for wide, long blindstitch and position fabric to right of needle. Stitch so left swing of needle stitches over folded edge and remaining stitches are on fabric. On some machines, blindstitch can be mirror-imaged, allowing you to position fabric and stitch as in step 2a.

3) Trim fabric from wrong side, close to stitching.

Edgestitched Finishes

An edgestitched finish is especially suitable for woven lingerie fabrics. It works well for the edges of a silky sleep shirt and for crisp edges on batiste lingerie, because it does not add excess bulk that could interfere with the drape of the fabric. For best results, stitch the edgestitched finish in-the-round.

Allow ⅜" (1 cm) seam or hem allowances on edges that will have edgestitched finishes.

How to Sew an Edgestitched Finish

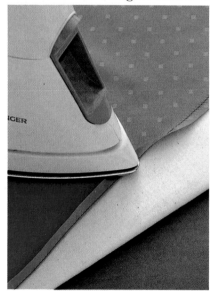

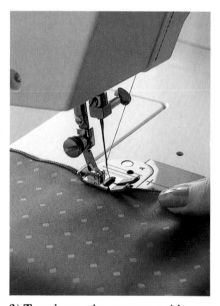

1) Machine-stitch ¼" (6 mm) from raw edge. Turn edge to wrong side on stitching line; press fold.

2) Stitch, using short stitch length, close to fold. Trim excess fabric close to stitching. Press to remove fullness if fabric has stretched.

3) Turn hem edge to wrong side, enclosing raw edge. Stitch an even distance from edge.

Bound Edge Finishes

A bound edge finish provides a versatile, stable edge that can be used on many fabrics, giving different effects. For example, use a contrasting satin binding to trim silky pajamas, or use matching fabric for a subtle edge on a cotton knit sleep shirt.

Bound edge finishes are sewn using flat or in-the-round construction; for either method, the ends of the finished binding are neatly enclosed. You may prefer the easier flat construction, unless you want to stitch all the seams of the garment for a fitting before the binding is applied. The ends of the binding can also be finished neatly on garments with closures at the neckline. The completed bias binding is ¼" (6 mm) wide.

How to Sew a Bound Edge Finish Using Flat Construction

1) **Cut** binding strip 1¾" (4.5 cm) wide by the length of edge to be bound plus ½" (1.3 cm); cut woven fabric on the bias, or cut knit fabric on crosswise grain. Strip may be pieced, if necessary. Trim seam or hem allowance from garment.

2) **Press** binding strip in half lengthwise, wrong sides together. Bias strips may stretch during pressing, so check that folded width is ⅞" (2.2 cm); reshape, if necessary. Place on right side of garment, raw edges even; pin. Stitch ¼" (6 mm) seam. Trim end of binding even with raw edge.

3) **Press** the binding away from garment, with seam allowances toward binding. Stitch final seam in garment. Trim seam allowances of final seam, if necessary, to reduce bulk at binding.

4) **Fold** binding around edge; press and pin or baste. Edgestitch on binding from right side of garment, catching folded edge on wrong side.

Curved lower edge. Follow steps 1 and 2. Press the binding away from the garment, with seam allowances toward binding. Fold and stitch binding as in step 4. Stitch final seam in garment, creating mitered effect.

How to Sew a Bound Edge Finish Using In-the-round Construction

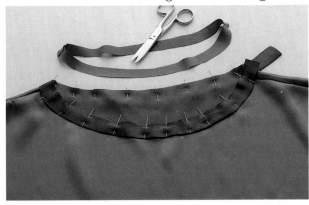

1) Cut bias strip 1¾" (4.5 cm) wide by length of edge to be bound plus 2" (1.3 cm). Trim seam allowance from garment. Press strip in half lengthwise, wrong sides together; pin to right side of garment, with raw edges even. Trim ends so they measure the same as width of folded binding.

2) Stitch ¼" (6 mm) seam, beginning and ending seam 3" (7.5 cm) from ends. Unfold binding. Fold ends diagonally, forming a square, and finger-press the seamline.

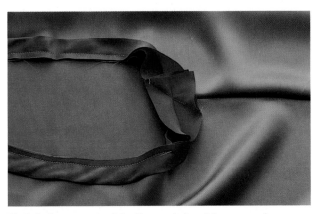

3) Stitch seam in binding, right sides together, matching finger-pressed seamlines; trim to ¼" (6 mm) and press open.

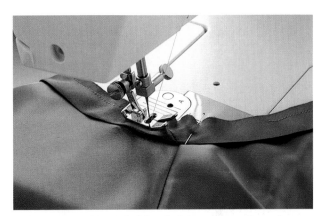

4) Refold binding. Finish stitching seam. Complete the bound edge as in step 4, opposite, for flat construction.

How to Sew a Bound Edge Finish on a Garment with a Closure

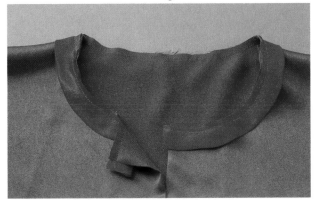

1) Follow step 1, opposite, for flat construction. Press binding strip in half lengthwise, wrong sides together; place on right side of garment, raw edges even, leaving ¼" (6 mm) seam allowance extending beyond garment opening on both ends. Stitch ¼" (6 mm) seam.

2) Press the binding away from garment, with seam allowances toward binding. Fold binding at ends, right sides together; stitch ¼" (6 mm) seam through all layers of binding. Trim seam allowances at end. Finish bound edge as in step 4, opposite, for flat construction.

Lace-trimmed Bound Edge Finishes

Lace-trimmed bound edge finishes are often used at the necklines and armholes of lightweight cotton lingerie, such as batiste camisoles and nightgowns. This decorative edge finish neatly encases the edge of the garment with a concealed binding. Use this technique for circular openings sewn in-the-round or for garments with closures.

How to Sew a Bound Edge with Narrow Lace Edging

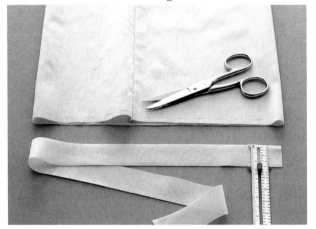

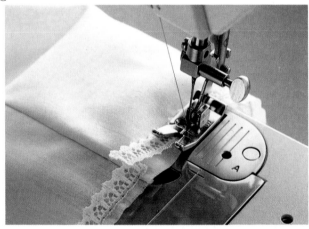

1) Cut bias strip 1" (2.5 cm) wide by length of edge to be bound plus ½" (1.3 cm) for finishing ends; for garment with closure, add 1" (2.5 cm) for finishing ends. Strips may be pieced, if necessary. Trim seam allowance of garment to ¼" (6 mm).

2) Position narrow lace edging on fabric, right sides together, with straight edge of lace ¼" (6 mm) from raw edge; overlap ends of lace ⅜" (1 cm) for in-the-round construction. Machine-baste lace to garment on straight edge of lace.

3) Press binding strip in half lengthwise, wrong sides together. Pin strip over lace, matching raw edges. Fold ¼" (6 mm) of binding back at beginning of strip.

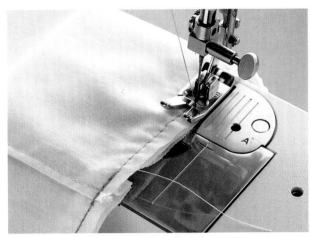

4) Lap other end of binding strip over folded end. Stitch over previous stitching.

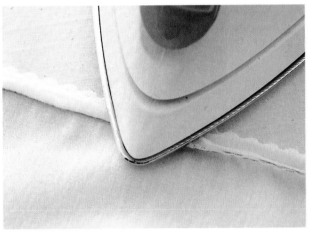

5) Trim seam allowances to ⅛" (3 mm). Press binding away from garment, with seam allowances toward the binding.

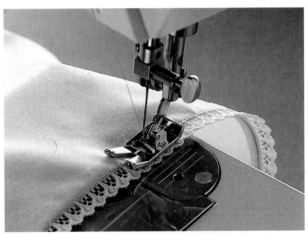

6) Press binding to inside of garment, extending lace. From right side, edgestitch close to seamline, through all layers. Zigzag through overlapped layers of lace; trim lace close to stitching.

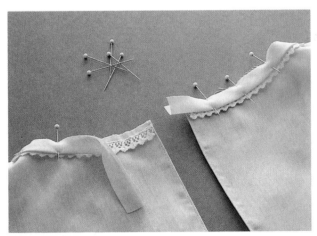

For garment with closure. 1) Follow steps 1 and 2, opposite. Press binding strip in half lengthwise, wrong sides together. Pin strip over lace, matching raw edges, with ½" (1.3 cm) seam allowance extending over edge of garment at each end.

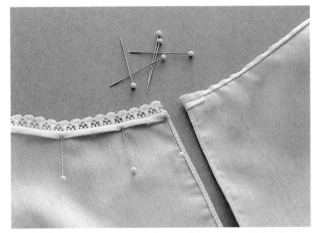

2) Stitch over previous stitching. Fold ends of binding strip around edges of garment opening. Stitch ends of binding in place. Finish bound edge as in steps 5 and 6, above.

Applying Lace

Lace adds a feminine touch to lingerie and may be used as an appliqué, edge finish, or insert. Select lace according to where the lace will be used and the type of fabric you are sewing (pages 16 and 17).

As their names imply, lace edgings are used at the edges of lingerie, and insertion laces are used for inserts. Galloon laces are versatile laces and can be used as either edge finishes or inserts.

Transparent tape may be used for quick positioning of lace without pins. After positioning the lace, stitch near the edge, through the tape, using a narrow zigzag stitch of medium length.

Lace Appliqués

Lace appliqués can become the focal point of a negligee or add just the right accent to intimate apparel. Although they are intricate in appearance, appliqués are fast and easy to apply.

You can coordinate lace appliqués with the lace trims you are using on a garment by cutting individual motifs, or groups of motifs, from the trim. Or you can use lace medallions, which are available in several types of lace and in a variety of shapes and sizes.

How to Make and Apply a Lace Appliqué

1) Cut motif from lace, leaving one or two rows of net around edges to prevent *cordonnets,* or cords, from raveling. Position appliqué on right side of fabric; tape or pin in place.

2) Stitch around outer edge, using narrow zigzag; stitch through tape, if used. Remove tape after stitching.

3) Trim fabric under lace from wrong side for sheer appliqué; trim woven fabric ⅛" (3 mm) away from stitches, or trim knit fabric close to stitches. For overlay effect, do not trim fabric under lace.

Lace Edges

Lace edgings and galloon laces add a delicate, finished edge to lingerie. They may be applied using either flat or in-the-round construction. The flat method of construction is faster, but use in-the-round construction for inconspicuous seams that do not interrupt the lace pattern.

It is not always possible to match motifs perfectly at the seams. However, because of the intricate pattern of lace, any differences in the repeat of the pattern are generally unnoticeable. Avoid stretching either the lace or the fabric when positioning the lace or stitching the seam. This is especially important if you are sewing bias-cut garments.

The basic method (upper left) for applying lace shows off the sheerness of the lace and may be used on knits or bias-cut wovens.

The overlay method (lower left) has a layer of garment fabric under the lace. When contrasting colors are used, the intricate detailing of the lace is emphasized.

The reinforced method (upper right) has two rows of stitching for added durability and is especially suitable as an edge finish for woven fabrics.

For the basic, overlay, and reinforced methods, the lace is placed on the fabric so the finished edge of the lace is aligned to the raw edge of the garment. Therefore, do not allow any hem allowances or seam allowances at this garment edge.

The overlock method (lower right) uses the overlock machine, or serger, to apply lace to straight edges, using either the flatlock stitch, shown above, or the 3-thread overlock stitch. Before applying the lace, subtract ¾" (2 cm) from the width of the lace and trim an amount equal to this measurement away from the raw edge of the garment. This allows for a 6 mm stitch width on the overlock machine and for trimming away ¼" (6 mm) of fabric at the edge with the overlock knives as you sew. The overlock method is not suitable for curved seams or corners.

How to Apply Lace Edging (flat construction)

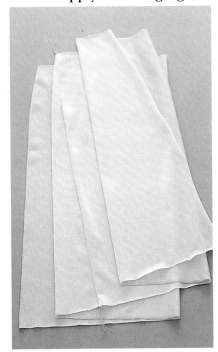

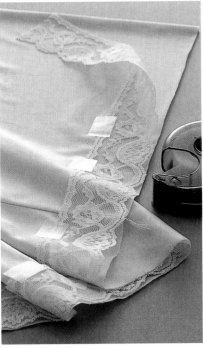

1) Stitch all but one seam at the garment opening; leave side seam or center back seam unstitched.

2) Tape or pin lace to the garment. Apply lace, using any of the methods on pages 43 to 45.

3) Stitch remaining seam, stitching through lace. Fold seam allowances to one side; stitch again through the lace.

How to Apply Lace Edging (in-the-round construction)

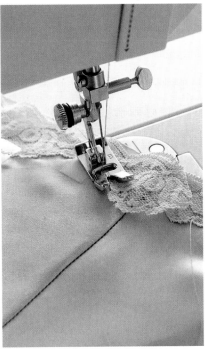

1) Stitch all seams at the garment opening. Tape or pin lace to the garment, planning the placement of lace motifs (page 42). Overlap ends of lace, leaving excess length.

2) Stitch lace to garment, using one of the methods on pages 43 to 45, stopping before lapped ends of lace. Trim the excess lace so ends overlap ⅜"(1 cm) at stitching line, cutting around motif. Continue stitching.

3) Stitch through the overlapped layers of lace, following motif. Trim excess lace close to stitching.

Tips for Planning Lace Placement

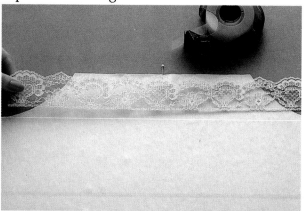

Experiment with placement of lace on garment edge to determine most desirable position of motifs. You may want to center a motif or scallop at center front or center back.

Plan to coordinate narrow lace edging with a wider one, to eliminate the need for mitering corners or matching motifs at seamlines.

Match motifs at seamline whenever possible. Lace may be eased slightly to the fabric to facilitate matching. Or, depending on the fit of the garment, it may be possible to adjust the width of the seam allowances in order to match the motifs.

Plan to stitch around the motif where the lace design blends, when it is not possible to match lace motifs at the seamline. The adjusted motif will appear either elongated or shortened.

Tips for Positioning Lace on Bias-cut Garments

Place bias-cut garment over pattern piece, aligning center front and seamlines; ease fabric to original size if it has stretched out of shape. Pin to padded surface, and pin or tape lace in place.

Measure edge of pattern piece, eliminating seam allowances. Mark this length on lace; leave excess at ends for matching motifs. Position lace edging on bias-cut fabric, easing fabric to fit lace.

How to Apply Lace Edging Using the Basic Method

1) Position lace on fabric, right sides up, matching scalloped edge of lace to raw edge of fabric; if using in-the-round construction, overlap ends of lace, leaving excess length. Tape or pin in place.

2) Stitch along inner edge of lace, using narrow zigzag; stitch through tape, if used.

3) Stop stitching before the lapped ends of lace if using in-the-round construction, and trim excess lace so ends overlap ⅜" (1 cm) at the stitching line, cutting around motif; continue stitching.

4) Trim knit fabric close to stitches from wrong side, or trim woven fabric ⅛" (3 mm) away from stitches.

5) Zigzag through overlapped layers of lace, following motif, if using in-the-round construction; trim excess lace close to stitching. Remove tape, if used, before pressing. (Contrasting thread was used to show detail.)

How to Apply Lace Edging Using the Overlay Method

1) Follow steps 1, 2, and 3 on page 43 for basic method. If using in-the-round construction, fold fabric under lace toward garment, and zigzag through overlapped layers of lace, following motif. Trim excess lace close to stitching.

2) Stitch through lace and fabric ¼" (6 mm) from outer edge of lace, using narrow zigzag. Trim knit fabric close to outer row of stitching from wrong side, or trim woven fabric ⅛" (3 mm) away from stitches. Remove tape, if used, before pressing.

How to Apply Lace Edging Using the Reinforced Method

1) Follow steps 1, 2, and 3 on page 43 for the basic method. Remove tape, if used. Trim hem allowance to ½" (1.3 cm); press toward garment, clipping curves as necessary.

2) Zigzag through overlapped layers of lace, following motif, if using in-the-round construction; trim excess lace close to stitching. Zigzag at upper edge of lace, from right side, over previous stitches. Trim fabric close to stitching.

3-thread overlock seam. 1) Adjust length of garment (page 40). Place lace on garment, right sides together, with straight edge of lace ¼" (6 mm) from raw edge of fabric; if using in-the-round construction, overlap ends, leaving excess length. Pin in place.

2) Stitch, using 3-thread overlock stitch, trimming fabric next to lace with overlock knives. If using in-the-round construction, stop stitching before lapped ends of lace, and trim excess lace so ends overlap ⅜" (1 cm) at stitching line, cutting around motif; continue stitching.

3) Zigzag, using a conventional machine, through overlapped layers of lace, following motif if using in-the-round construction; trim the excess lace close to stitching.

Flatlock seam. Apply lace as in steps 1 to 3, above, except use flatlock stitch and place lace and fabric *wrong* sides together. Thread should match lace, because it will show on right side of garment. Pull flatlock seam flat.

Lace Edges with Corners & Curves

Lace can be easily applied at corners and along the curved edges of lingerie garments. Three methods may be used to apply the lace: the basic, the overlay, and the reinforced.

When lace is used at corners, it can be mitered, or the ends of the lace can be joined at a corner, stitching diagonally to give the appearance of mitering. The ends of the lace may also be joined by stitching across the corner following a motif.

Lace can be shaped to follow curved edges. Whenever possible, shape the lace by pressing it with a steam iron. If a wide lace is used, it may be necessary to clip the lace next to some of the motifs and overlap the edges until the lace lies smooth and flat. After shaping the lace to follow the curved edge, zigzag along the clipped edges to secure them. The zigzag stitches follow along the edge of the motifs, making them nearly invisible.

How to Miter Lace Edging at an Outside Corner

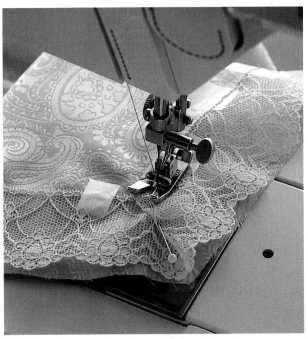

1) Fold lace, right sides together, matching either the scallops or the motifs. Place lace on right side of fabric, positioning foldline at outer edge of lace at corner of garment. Match scalloped edge of lace to raw edge of garment. Tape or pin bottom layer of lace in place.

2) Place scalloped edge of lace along remaining raw edge of fabric, folding lace at corner to miter. Tape or pin in place. Stitch along inner edge of lace, using narrow zigzag; stitch through tape, if used.

3a) Basic method. Trim knit fabric close to the stitches, or trim woven fabric ⅛" (3 mm) away from stitches. Stitch across corner through layers of lace, from right side, using narrow zigzag; trim excess lace close to stitching. Remove tape.

3b) Overlay method. Fold fabric under lace toward garment. Stitch across corner through layers of lace; trim excess lace close to stitching. Stitch on outer edge and trim fabric as for overlay method on page 44, step 2. Remove tape.

3c) Reinforced method. Remove tape, if used. Press fabric under lace toward garment, clipping curves as necessary. Stitch across corner through layers of lace; trim excess lace close to stitching. Zigzag along edge of lace, from right side. Trim excess fabric.

How to Miter Lace Edging at an Inside Corner

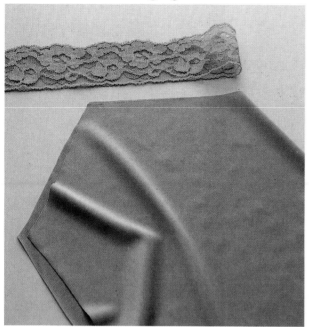

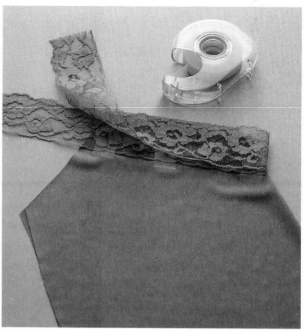

Basic or reinforced method. 1) Fold fabric wrong sides together at inside corner, matching raw edges. Fold lace, right sides together, matching scallops or motifs.

2) Place scalloped edge of folded lace along raw edge of fabric, so foldline at inner edge of lace is aligned to foldline of fabric. Secure bottom layer of lace to fabric, using tape.

3) Unfold fabric and lace. Place scalloped edge of the lace along the remaining raw edge of the fabric, folding lace at corner to miter. Tape or pin in place.

4) Stitch along inner edge of lace, using narrow zigzag; stitch through tape, if used. Finish as for mitered outside corner on page 47, following step 3a or 3c.

Overlay method. Follow steps 1, 2, and 3, above. Remove tape as necessary at corner; stitch across lace at corner from right side. Trim lace close to stitching. Reposition tape. Stitch along inner edge of lace, using narrow zigzag; stitch through tape, if used. Stitch on outer edge as on page 44, step 2.

How to Join the Ends of Lace Edging at an Outside Corner

1) Position the lace on the fabric, right sides up, aligning motifs at ends of lace at the corner. Tape or pin in place.

2) Stitch along inner edge of lace, using narrow zigzag; stitch through tape, if used. Finish as for outside corner on page 47, step 3a, 3b, or 3c; stitching across corner may follow motif or may be diagonal straight line.

How to Join the Ends of Lace Edging at an Inside Corner

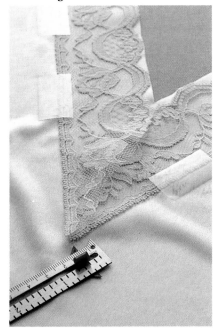

Basic or reinforced method. 1) Position lace on fabric, right sides up, aligning scallops or motifs at ends of lace at corner. Tape or pin in place. Trim lace so ends overlap ⅜" (1 cm) at corner.

2) Stitch along inner edge of lace, using narrow zigzag; stitch through tape, if used. Finish as for mitered outside corner on page 47, step 3a or 3c; stitching across corner may follow motif, if desired.

Overlay method. Follow step 1, left. Remove tape as necessary at corner; stitch across lace at corner; stitching may follow motif, if desired. Trim lace close to stitching. Reposition tape. Stitch along inner edge of lace, using narrow zigzag; stitch through tape, if used. Stitch on outer edge as on page 44, step 2.

How to Apply Wide Lace Edging on Outside Curves

1) Position lace on fabric, right sides up, matching scalloped edge of lace to raw edge of fabric; lace will not lie smooth on inner edge. Shape curve as much as possible with steam. Tape or pin in place.

2) Clip the lace from inner edge, following motifs, as necessary to overlap and flatten lace. Tape or pin lace in place.

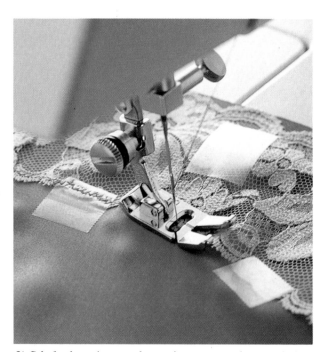

3) Stitch along inner edge, using narrow zigzag; stitch through tape, if used.

4a) Basic method. Trim knit fabric close to stitches from wrong side, or trim woven fabric ⅛" (3 mm) away from stitches. Stitch through overlapped layers of lace, following motifs, using narrow zigzag. Remove tape. Trim excess lace close to stitching.

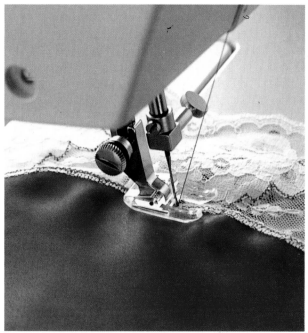

4b) Overlay method. Fold fabric under lace toward garment. Stitch through overlapped layers of lace, following motifs, using narrow zigzag; trim excess lace close to stitching. Stitch on outer edge and trim fabric as for overlay method on page 44, step 2.

4c) Reinforced method. Remove tape, if used. Press fabric under lace toward garment, clipping curves as necessary. Stitch through overlapped layers of lace, following motifs, using narrow zigzag; trim excess lace close to stitching. Zigzag along edge of lace, from right side; trim excess fabric.

How to Apply Wide Lace Edging on Inside Curves

1) Position lace on fabric, right sides up, matching scalloped edge of lace to raw edge of fabric; lace will not lie smooth on outer edge. Shape curve as much as possible with steam. Tape or pin in place.

2) Clip the lace from outer edge, following motifs, as necessary to overlap and flatten lace. Tape or pin in place.

3) Stitch along inner edge, using narrow zigzag; stitch through tape, if used. Finish as for outside curves, opposite, following step 4a, 4b, or 4c.

Lace Inserts

Lace can be inserted at any location on a garment without adjusting the pattern. It is not necessary to use an insertion lace with straight edges; galloon laces, which have scalloped edges, also make attractive inserts. The basic, overlay, and reinforced methods are used for adding lace inserts. Either flat or in-the-round construction works well.

A lace insert can add a finishing touch to a garment with a hem when the lace is positioned at the top of the hem. Cut the garment the finished length plus the desired width of the hem and half the width of the lace. The lace is applied as you stitch the hem. When adding a lace insert at the hem, use either the basic or the overlay method; the reinforced method should not be used because the hem would have too much bulk.

How to Sew a Lace Insert Using the Basic Method

1) Plan placement of lace insert. Position lace on fabric, right sides up. Overlap ends, leaving excess length if using in-the-round construction. Tape or pin lace in place.

2) Stitch along both edges of lace, using narrow zigzag and stitching through tape, if used; stop stitching before lapped ends of lace if using in-the-round construction. Complete as on page 43, steps 3, 4, and 5.

How to Sew a Lace Insert Using the Overlay Method

1) Position lace as in step 1, opposite. Stitch along one edge of lace, using narrow zigzag; stitch through tape, if used. If using in-the-round construction, complete step 3 on page 43. Fold fabric away from the lace, removing tape as necessary. Zigzag through overlapped ends of lace; trim excess lace close to stitching.

2) Reposition fabric under lace, and stitch through lace and fabric along other edge of lace, using narrow zigzag. Remove tape, if used; press. (Contrasting thread was used to show detail.)

How to Sew a Lace Insert Using the Reinforced Method

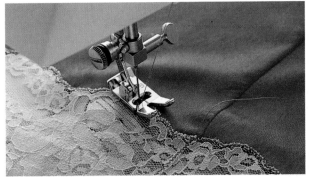

1) Position lace as in step 1, opposite. Stitch along both edges of lace, using narrow zigzag; stitch through tape, if used. If using in-the-round construction, complete step 3 on page 43. Trim fabric ¼" to ½" (6 mm to 1.3 cm) from stitching on both sides; press toward garment, clipping curves as necessary.

2) Zigzag through overlapped ends of lace, following motif, if using in-the-round construction; trim excess lace close to stitching. Zigzag along both long edges of lace from right side. Trim fabric close to stitching.

How to Sew a Lace Insert at a Hem

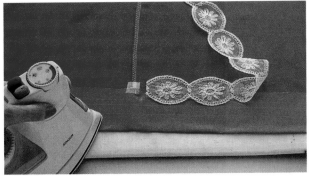

1) Fold the lower edge of the garment to wrong side, an amount equal to the desired width of hem plus half the width of lace; tape or pin in place. Press lower edge, but do not press over tape.

2) Position lace on garment, right sides up, the desired width of hem away from the foldline; if using in-the-round construction, overlap ends, leaving excess length. Tape or pin in place. Stitch and trim as for basic method, opposite, or overlay method, above. (Contrasting thread was used to show detail.)

Applying Elastic

Elastic may be applied using either flat or in-the-round construction. Although flat construction is faster, elastic applied in-the-round has a neater finish and the joined ends of the elastic are less bulky. When stretching the elastic as you sew, use a medium-to-long zigzag stitch so the elastic will return to its original length when relaxed. If the stitches are too short, the thread buildup prevents the elastic from recovering completely.

There are several methods for applying elastic, each having a different finished appearance. The method you select depends not only on the look you want to create, but also on the type of elastic and fabric you are using. Select the elastic and cut the length recommended for the garment opening (page 18).

If you are using an application method different from the one recommended on the pattern, it may be necessary to adjust the seam allowance of the pattern. For example, if you are using the reinforced method for applying elastic and the pattern is designed for a casing, adjust the seam allowance on the pattern from the foldline of the casing to the cutting line.

The reinforced method, recommended for either knits or wovens, is a durable method for applying lingerie elastic in-the-round. This technique is preferred when you have lingerie elastic that matches or coordinates with the fabric. The elastic may be applied so it is exposed on the right side of the garment and the fabric is next to the skin. Or it may be applied so only the picot edge shows on the right side of the garment. The seam allowance for this method is equal to the width of the elastic.

The overlock method, used for applying lingerie elastics to all fabrics, is a durable, one-step method sewn on the serger. The flatlock stitch or the 3-thread overlock stitch may be used, and the elastic may be applied using either flat or in-the-round construction. The seam allowance for this method is ¼" (6 mm).

The overlap method is a fast technique used for applying stretch lace, using either flat or in-the-round construction. It may also be used for applying lingerie elastic. It works best for knits, such as tricot, but may be used on bias-cut wovens. No seam allowance is required for this method; trim the seam allowance for the elasticized edge from the pattern before cutting the garment.

The covered method completely covers the elastic with fabric and is used for applying elastic in-the-round to any fabric. This method uses regular elastic, such as cotton swimwear elastic, which has good stretch and recovery. The covered method is especially good when you are sewing woven fabrics or when it is not possible to find lingerie elastic in a color that coordinates with the fabric. The seam allowance for this method is equal to twice the width of the elastic.

The casing method is also used when you want to completely cover elastic with fabric and is used for applying regular elastic in-the-round to any fabric type. Although this method is somewhat bulkier than the covered method, it is used when you want to avoid stretching and stitching through the elastic as you sew or when you want to adjust the length of the elastic after it is inserted. The casing allowance for ¼" (6 mm) elastic is ¾" (2 cm).

The binding method, stitched in-the-round, allows you to cover elastic with a matching or contrasting knit binding. Transparent elastic may be used for this technique to minimize bulk. No seam allowance is required for this method; trim the seam allowance for the elasticized edge from the pattern before cutting the garment.

How to Apply Elastic (flat construction)

1) Stitch all but one seam at the garment opening, backstitching at ends; leave side seam of panties or side seam or center back seam of half slip unstitched. Divide elastic and garment edge into fourths; pin-mark. Pin elastic to garment, matching markings.

2) Apply elastic, using a method recommended for flat construction, above. Stitch remaining seam, stitching through elastic. Fold seam allowances to one side, and stitch again through elastic.

Elastic applications: (top to bottom, left) reinforced exposed, reinforced hidden, 3-thread overlock; (top to bottom, right) overlap, covered, casing, binding.

How to Apply Elastic (in-the-round construction)

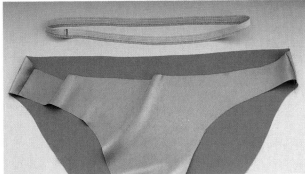

1) Stitch all seams at garment opening, backstitching at ends. Overlap ends of elastic ¼" (6 mm); tape in place to secure, if desired. Stitch back and forth through tape and elastic, using zigzag stitch of medium width and length.

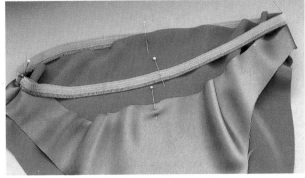

2) Divide elastic and garment opening into fourths; pin-mark. Pin elastic to garment, matching markings. Place elastic seam at side seam of panties or at side seam or center back seam of half slip. Apply elastic, using any method (pages 56 to 59).

How to Apply Lingerie Elastic Using the Reinforced Method

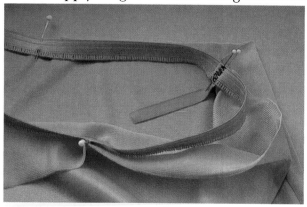

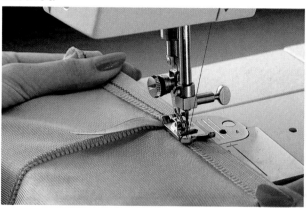

Exposed elastic. 1) Stitch ends of elastic together if using in-the-round construction, as on page 55, step 1. Divide elastic and garment edge into fourths; pin-mark. Pin elastic to fabric, *wrong* sides together, with straight edge of elastic even with raw edge; match pin marks. If desired, place ½" (1.3 cm) satin ribbon under joined ends of elastic, matching raw edges.

2) Stitch close to picot edge of elastic, using zigzag stitch of narrow width and medium length. Stretch elastic to fit the fabric as you sew, taking care not to stretch the fabric.

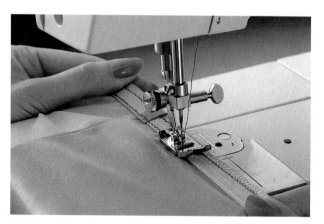

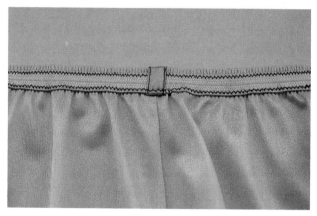

3) Trim fabric from right side close to stitches. Turn elastic to right side. Fold ribbon around elastic, trimming as necessary. Zigzag close to straight edge of elastic, stretching as you sew.

4) Stitch close to edges of satin ribbon to encase ends of the elastic. Steam elastic back to original shape, if necessary; do not touch elastic with iron.

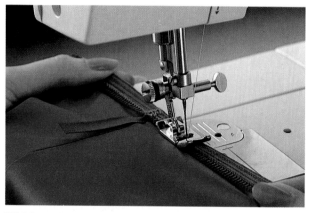

Hidden elastic. 1) Stitch elastic as in steps 1 and 2, above, except pin elastic to fabric, *right* sides together. Trim fabric from wrong side close to stitches.

2) Turn elastic to wrong side, folding ribbon around elastic. Zigzag close to straight edge of the elastic, stretching as you sew, or use wide 3-step zigzag stitch for fluted effect. Finish ribbon as in step 4, above.

How to Apply Lingerie Elastic Using the Overlock Method

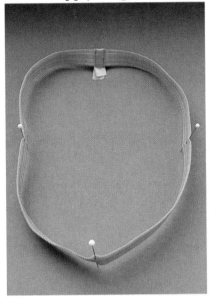

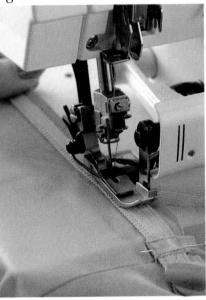

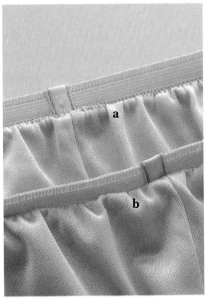

1) Stitch ends of elastic together if using in-the-round construction, as on page 55, step 1. If desired, fold ribbon around elastic, as shown, covering ends; edgestitch near edges of ribbon, using a conventional machine. Divide elastic and garment edge into fourths; pin-mark.

2) Pin elastic to garment, right sides together, with straight edge of elastic ¼" (6 mm) from raw edge of fabric; match pin marks. Stitch, using flatlock stitch or 3-thread overlock stitch. Stretch elastic to fit fabric as you sew; do not cut elastic with overlock knives.

3) Pull seam flat if using flatlock stitch **(a)**; ladder of stitches shows on right side of fabric. If 3-thread overlock stitch **(b)** is used, seam is slightly bulkier, but stitches are hidden on the inside of the garment. Steam elastic back to original shape, if necessary; do not touch elastic with iron.

How to Apply Stretch Lace or Lingerie Elastic Using the Overlap Method

1) Stitch ends of elastic together if using in-the-round construction, as on page 55, step 1. Divide elastic and garment edge into fourths; pin-mark. Pin elastic to garment, right sides up, with upper edge of stretch lace or picot edge of lingerie elastic even with raw edge; match pin marks. Stitch along lower edge, using zigzag stitch of medium width and length, stretching elastic to fit the fabric.

2) Trim fabric from wrong side, close to stitches if using knit fabric. For woven fabric, trim ⅛" (3 mm) from stitches. Steam elastic back to original shape, if necessary; do not touch elastic with iron.

How to Apply Regular Elastic Using the Covered Method

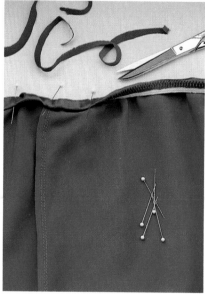

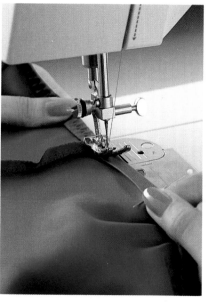

1) Stitch ends of elastic together if using in-the-round construction, as on page 55, step 1. Divide elastic and garment edge into fourths; pin-mark. Pin elastic to wrong side of garment, with edge of elastic even with raw edge; match pin marks. Stitch close to lower edge, using zigzag stitch, stretching elastic to fit the fabric as you sew.

2) Trim fabric from right side, close to stitches. Fold elastic twice to the wrong side of the garment.

3) Stitch close to lower edge of elastic, using wide, long 3-step zigzag or medium-to-long zigzag stitch; stretch as you sew. Steam elastic back to original shape, if necessary; do not touch elastic with iron.

How to Apply Regular Elastic Using the Casing Method

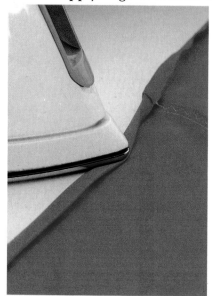

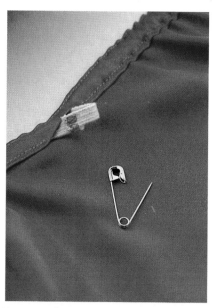

1) Fold under ¼" (6 mm) at edge of garment; press. Fold under and press ⅜" (1 cm) from first foldline.

2) Edgestitch close to outer edge; then stitch ¼" (6 mm) from first row of stitches for bias-cut garment, leaving an opening at center back. For garment cut on straight of grain, edgestitch close to both foldlines, leaving an opening.

3) Insert ¼" (6 mm) elastic through the casing, using small safety pin. Check fit, and stitch ends of elastic together, as on page 55, step 1; stitch opening closed.

How to Apply Transparent or Regular Elastic Using the Binding Method

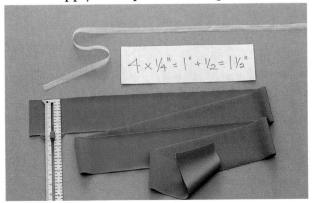

1) **Cut** binding strip from knit fabric, on crosswise grain, four times the width of elastic plus ½" (1.3 cm) by the length of garment opening plus ½" (1.3 cm).

2) **Pin** binding strip to garment edge, right sides together, with raw edges even. Fold ¼" (6 mm) seam allowance on binding at beginning of seam. Stitch binding to garment ¼" (6 mm) from edge, using long, narrow zigzag stitches.

3) **Overlap** ends of binding ¼" (6 mm) at end of seam; if binding has stretched during stitching, excess length may be trimmed.

4) **Stitch** ends of elastic together, as on page 55, step 1. Divide elastic and garment edge into fourths; pin-mark. Place elastic on wrong side of binding, with edge of elastic even with raw edge. Stitch close to lower edge, using long, narrow zigzag stitch, stretching elastic to fit the fabric as you sew.

5) **Trim** binding and garment edge from wrong side, close to stitching.

6) **Fold** binding over elastic to wrong side of garment; pin. Zigzag close to lower edge, stretching as you sew. Trim excess binding on wrong side. Steam elastic back to original shape, if necessary; do not touch elastic with iron.

Intimate Apparel

Half slip styles: (left to right) picot edge finish, edgestitched finish, galloon lace finish, galloon lace cut in half, tulip-style, slit opening.

Half Slips

Half slips are so fast and easy to sew, you may want to make several, in different styles and lengths. Slips may be straight, A-line, slightly flared, or full.

Silky fabrics, such as tricot and charmeuse, are frequently used for slips. When using tricot or other knits, lay out the pattern so the stretch of the knit will go around the body. For woven fabrics, lay out the pattern on the bias to give a soft drape and to provide some stretch for movement.

For slips made from knits or bias-cut wovens, 2" (5 cm) of ease is adequate at the hipline and gives a smooth fit without excess bulk. Patterns for fuller styles may include more ease. Length adjustments are made at the lower edge of the pattern.

The lower edge of a slip may be trimmed with lace, or hemmed with an edgestitched finish or picot edge finish. A slip may have a slit opening trimmed with lace (pages 64 and 65), positioned either at the side seam or at the center front or back. The basic techniques on pages 24 to 59 are used for sewing the seams and edge finishes, and for applying lace and elastic.

Lace and elastic may be applied to the slip using either flat or in-the-round construction. Or you may prefer a combination of the two methods, using the easier flat method to apply the lace, then attaching the elastic in-the-round for a smoother feel at the waistline. When lace is used as a trim, it is usually applied before the elastic, so the fabric can be smoothed out while you are positioning the lace.

Half Slips with Mitered Slit Openings

Sew a slip with a slit opening to wear with a button-front skirt or a skirt that has a back vent or side slit. The slit opening in the slip may be positioned at the side seam, center front, or center back.

A mitered slit opening is easy to sew and can be trimmed with either a lace edging or a galloon lace. The mitered corners at the lower edge of the slip are 1" (2.5 cm) apart to prevent the slip from showing at the skirt opening.

The instructions shown here are for the basic method of applying lace, using either flat or in-the-round construction. For the overlay or reinforced methods, refer to pages 47 to 49.

How to Sew a Half Slip with a Mitered Slit Opening

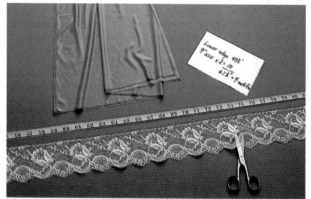

1) Stitch all but one seam if using flat construction, or stitch all seams if using in-the-round construction. Cut lace equal to distance around lower edge of slip plus twice the length of slit plus at least four extra motifs for matching.

2) Mark slit placement line perpendicular to lower edge, estimating finished length of slit. Fold lace, right sides together, at center of a scallop or between two scallops, allowing enough lace so end will extend to nearest seam. Position lace with fold ½" (1.3 cm) from placement line and with scallops along lower edge; tape or pin in place.

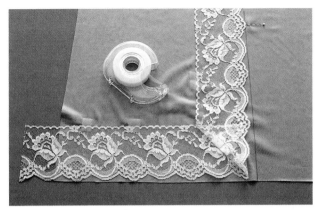

3) Miter corner by folding lace diagonally; position lace for first side of slit so center of a scallop is at or near top of placement line; the slit may need to be shortened or lengthened so lace scallops will match on both sides of slit.

4) Fold lace *under* diagonally at top of slit, aligning center of scallop to placement line; tape or pin.

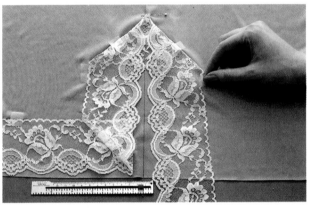

5) Fold lace *over* diagonally, then down second side of slit, so scallops are directly opposite the first side; right side of lace will face up. Tape or pin in place, with lace ½" (1.3 cm) away from placement line at lower edge of slip.

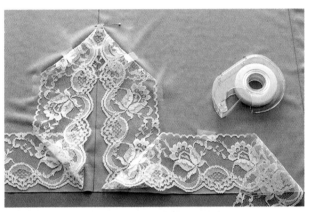

6) Miter lace at final corner; tape or pin in place. Tape or pin lace along remainder of lower edge.

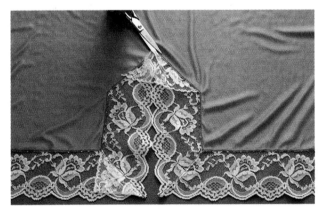

7) Stitch along inner edge of lace; trim fabric close to stitching from wrong side. Stitch diagonally across corners at lower edge, using narrow zigzag stitch; trim excess lace from wrong side.

8) Stitch final seam if using flat construction. Or zigzag through overlapped ends of lace, following motif, if using in-the-round construction; trim excess lace close to stitching. Apply elastic to upper edge of slip (pages 54 to 59).

Tulip-style Half Slips

A tulip-style half slip is easy to sew, and you do not need a pattern. Trimmed with lace, the opening is gently curved so the slip does not show at buttoned openings or vents in skirts. For easier application, use a narrow lace, which can be steamed to the curved shape. If a wide lace is used, shape the lace as on page 50.

To make a tulip-style slip, cut a straight-grain rectangle of knit or woven fabric the width of the hip measurement plus 4" (10 cm) for ease. For the length, measure from the waist to the desired length of the slip and add the seam allowance required for applying the elastic.

On the opposite page, the lace is applied using the basic method. For the overlay or the reinforced methods, refer to pages 50 and 51. When an edging lace, which has one straight edge, is used with woven fabric, the reinforced method is recommended to prevent the fabric from raveling when trimmed on the straight of grain next to the straight edge of the lace.

How to Sew a Tulip-style Half Slip

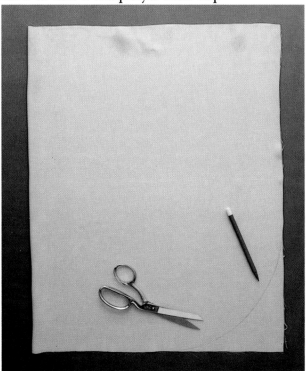

1) Fold fabric in half lengthwise. Round off corners at lower edge of slip, opposite folded edge, cutting through both layers.

2) Pin lace to sides and lower edge of slip, right sides up, aligning scalloped edge of lace to raw edge of fabric. Shape lace around curves, using steam; tape in place.

3) Zigzag along inner edge of lace. Remove tape, if used. Trim fabric close to stitching from wrong side.

4) Overlap lace at front edges, right sides up. Pin in place 7" to 10" (18 to 25.5 cm) down from upper edge; zigzag along edges of overlapped lace. Apply elastic to upper edge of slip (pages 54 to 59).

Full Slips & Camisoles

The bodice styles of full slips and camisoles vary considerably, from the straight lines of the chemise to the form fit of the Empire style and the continuous curves of the princess style (shown left to right).

Full slips and camisoles that fit well are more flattering to the figure and more comfortable to wear. Well-fitted slips and camisoles also contribute to a smooth fit in the dresses or blouses that are worn over them. If you wear a B-cup or smaller, select a pattern by your full bust measurement. If you wear a C-cup or larger, select a pattern by your high bust measurement to prevent gaping at the upper edge of the slip; it will be necessary, however, to adjust the pattern in the full bust area (pages 70 and 71).

The correct back waist length is important to achieve a good fit. Compare your back waist length (page 13) to the back waist length printed on the pattern envelope. If the difference is more than ½" (1.3 cm), you will need to adjust the pattern as shown below; when a back waist length adjustment is needed, the pattern front is always adjusted in length to correspond to the pattern back. This adjustment should be made before any other pattern adjustments.

Fabric choices for full slips and camisoles are similar to those for half slips. Tricot and silky fabrics like charmeuse are frequently used; fine cotton knits and batistes are also appropriate.

To provide adequate wearing ease, cut pattern pieces from knit fabrics so the crosswise grain goes around the body; cut pattern pieces from woven fabrics on the bias. The lower edge of a full slip or camisole is finished the same as the lower edge of a half slip (pages 63 to 65).

How to Make a Back Waist Length Pattern Adjustment

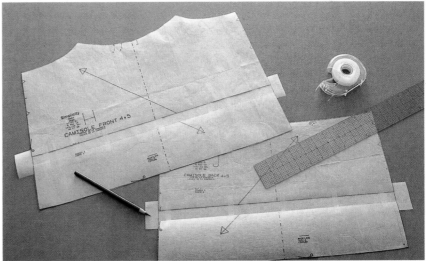

Draw lines on back and front pattern pieces, 2" (5 cm) above waistline and perpendicular to center front and center back; cut apart on marked lines. If your back waist length is longer than pattern measurement, spread pattern pieces an amount equal to difference between measurements. If your back waist length is shorter than pattern, lap pattern pieces. Tape pattern in place, adding tissue paper if pattern is being spread. Draw new cutting lines and seamlines.

How to Adjust a Chemise-style Bodice for a Full Bust

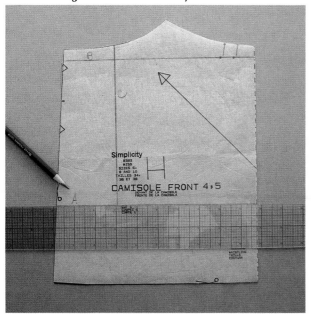

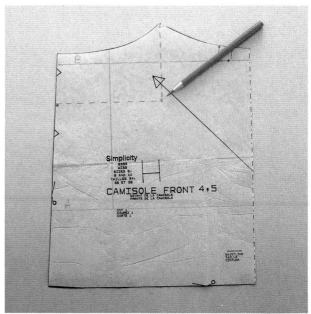

1) Draw Line A on pattern front as for back waist length adjustment (page 69). Draw Line B ½" (1.3 cm) down from underarm and perpendicular to center front. Draw Line C parallel to center front, midway between side seam and strap placement mark, ending at Line A. For full-size pattern, use only one-half of the pattern piece.

2) Mark bust point at intersection of vertical line through strap placement mark and horizontal line through center of ease area at side seam; if pattern has a dart, it will point to the bust point.

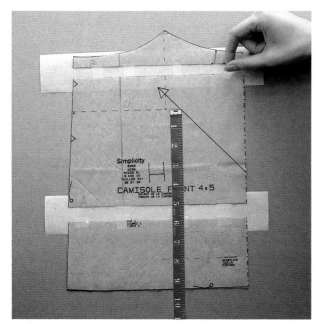

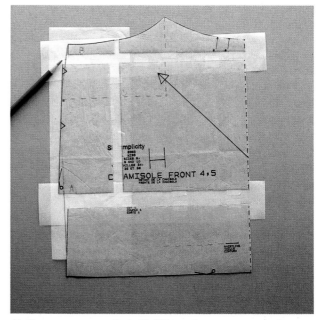

3) Cut pattern on Lines A and B. Make back waist length adjustment at Line A, if necessary (page 69). Compare measurement of pattern, from bust point to waistline, to body measurement (page 13). Spread the pattern along Line B an amount equal to the difference; tape pattern in place, adding tissue paper.

4) Cut pattern on line C. Place tissue paper under pattern. Spread middle side section along Line C, ½" (1.3 cm) for C-cup, ¾" (2 cm) for D-cup, or 1" (2.5 cm) for DD-cup. Spread the upper side section along line C, half the distance the middle section was moved. Tape pattern in place. Draw new cutting lines to resemble original lines. Make full-size pattern, if desired. Gather extra fullness in bust area when sewing garment.

How to Adjust an Empire-style Bodice for a Full Bust

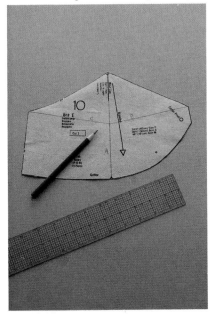

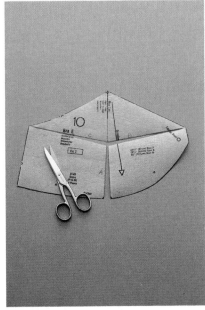

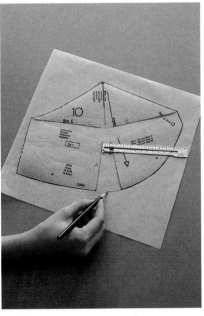

1) Draw Line A from placement mark for straps through center of ease on lower edge of bodice. Draw Line B from midpoint of Line A to upper edge at center front line. Draw Line C from midpoint of Line A to upper edge at side seam.

2) Cut on Line A from lower edge of bodice to midpoint of Line A. Cut on Lines B and C to, but not through, outer edges of pattern.

3) Place tissue paper under pattern. Spread pattern at bust point, ½" (1.3 cm) for C-cup, ¾" (2 cm) for D-cup, or 1" (2.5 cm) for DD-cup. Tape pattern in place. Draw curved cutting line on tissue at lower edge.

How to Adjust a Princess-style Bodice for a Full Bust

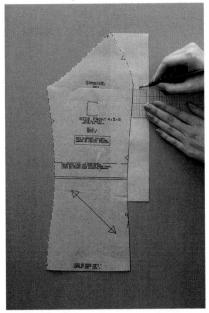

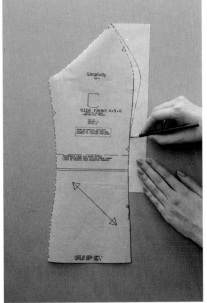

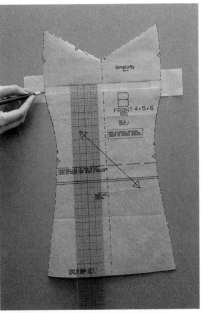

1) Tape tissue paper under side front pattern. Measure out from cutting line at fullest part of bustline curve, and mark tissue to add ½" (1.3 cm) for C-cup, ¾" (2 cm) for D-cup, or 1" (2.5 cm) for DD-cup.

2) Draw new cutting line from mark at bustline, tapering to original cutting line at upper edge and 4" (10 cm) below mark.

3) Draw horizontal line on center front pattern at the fullest part of bustline curve; cut on marked line. Spread pattern same amount added in step 1, adding tissue paper. Tape in place. Draw new cutting line in adjustment area.

Straps for Full Slips & Camisoles

You can choose from several types of straps for slips and camisoles, from narrow spaghetti straps with a delicate appearance to wider straps that can better conceal bra straps. For quick and easy straps, stretch lace may be used. Or sew self-fabric straps in only a few minutes.

Tube straps made from fabric can be any width. Narrow tubes, called spaghetti straps, are especially popular on full slips and camisoles.

Picot straps, made from tricot, have gently scalloped edges. The rounded type is a narrow strap similar to a spaghetti strap, but has a fluted effect. The wrong side of the fabric will show on the rounded picot straps, although any difference between the right and wrong side of the fabric is unnoticeable due to the picot effect. The flat picot strap, which fits smoothly under clothing, is wider than the rounded strap. Both types coordinate well with the picot edge finishes on pages 30 and 31.

Before stitching straps to the slip or camisole, pin them in place with small safety pins and try on the garment to check the fit.

How to Make Tube Straps

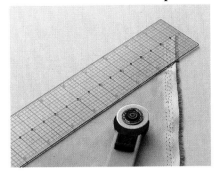

1) Cut fabric strip twice as wide as the desired finished width plus ½" (1.3 cm) for seam allowances; cut woven fabrics on the bias, or cut knits on lengthwise grainline.

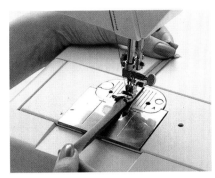

2) Fold strip in half lengthwise, right sides together. Stitch ¼" (6 mm) seam, using straight stitch, stretching fabric as you sew.

3) Trim seam allowances to finished width of strap if the strap will be narrower than ¼" (6 mm). Insert loop turner into fabric tube; secure latch hook to the seam allowances. Pull on loop turner, turning tube right side out.

How to Make Picot Straps

Rounded. Cut tricot on crosswise grain, ¾" (2 cm) wide and 3" (7.5 cm) longer than the finished length. Right side up, stretch fabric tightly so the edges roll; using wide, long zigzag, stitch over fabric, taking care not to catch fabric in stitches. Trim ends.

Flat. 1) Cut tricot on lengthwise grain, twice as wide as desired finished width plus ½" (1.3 cm) for seam allowances and 3" (7.5 cm) longer than desired finished length. Make tube strap, above, lightly pressing seam allowances open before turning tube right side out.

2) Center seamline on underside of strap, keeping seam allowances open; press. Stitch along both edges, using the picot edge finish (pages 30 and 31).

Tips for Attaching Straps

Zigzag strap to both fabric and lace edging. The two rows of stitches add strength and prevent lace from becoming damaged due to stress.

Stitch in the ditch, using straight stitch, if the upper edge of slip or camisole has a bound edge finish.

Sew straps and edge finishes from one piece of stretch lace. Apply stretch lace to back and underarm, using basic method (page 43). At front, lace continues, forming strap; stitch ends to garment back.

More Ideas for Full Slips & Camisoles

Lace trims and appliqués can add a pretty finish to the bodices of full slips and camisoles. Galloon lace can be positioned over the seamlines of an Empire-style full slip. Even after the fabric and seams under the lace are trimmed away, the bodice retains its shape.

Or simply center a symmetrical lace medallion at the upper edge of a chemise camisole. Then embellish the medallion by embroidering it with satin stitching and straight stitching along the design lines of the motif. Depending on the color of thread selected, this can add a touch of color to lace trims or can coordinate a neutral-colored lace to the fabric.

Lace can also be embellished with hand beading. Select small beads to prevent bulkiness under lightweight outer garments.

Creative Ideas for Bodices of Full Slips and Camisoles

Embroidered lace. Baste tear-away stabilizer to wrong side of lace. From right side, straight-stitch, using short stitches, or satin stitch, using closely spaced zigzag stitches; use colored threads and follow lines of lace motifs, as desired. Remove stabilizer by tearing it close to stitches.

Lace-trimmed bodice seams. Apply lace over seamlines of bodice, using basic method for inserts (page 52). Trim away fabric, including seams, under lace.

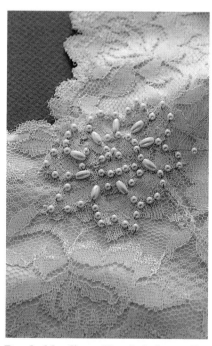

Beaded bodices. Handstitch small beads to the bodice of a camisole, positioning them to emphasize lace design.

Panties

Panties of all styles are easy to sew, using either flat or in-the-round construction. You may want to sew a lacy silk pantie or a cotton pantie with decorative brief elastic. Briefs, bikinis, hipsters, and high-cut panties are all sewn using the same basic techniques. French bikinis (pages 82 to 85) require special sewing techniques and offer more variety in styles.

Whatever the style, select the pattern size according to the hip measurement. Before laying out the pattern, decide which methods you will use for applying elastic or lace edge finishes. It may be necessary to adjust the seam allowances of the pattern, depending on the methods selected. Cut the elastic according to the guidelines on page 18.

Panties can be embellished with lace inserts and lace motifs. The lace is usually applied to the garment section before the panties are sewn, making it easier to keep the fabric smooth as you stitch. Instead of the usual lingerie elastics, stretch laces and brief elastics may be used for variety. Stretch lace is often used for bikinis because it provides a smooth fit.

Cotton single knit fabric works well for the crotch lining, because it is absorbent, breathes well, and is lightweight. Because dyes may cause an allergic reaction, white cotton knit is a good choice.

How to Sew a Lined Crotch with Enclosed Seams

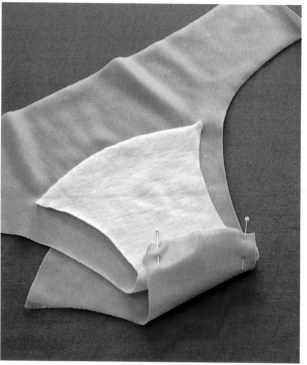

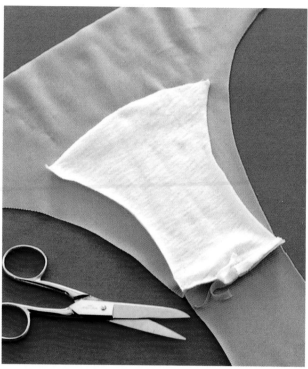

1) Align the crotch piece to pantie front, right sides together, matching centers and ends. Place crotch lining, right side down, on wrong side of pantie front. Pin layers together, with raw edges even.

2) Stitch seam through all layers of fabric; trim seam allowances to 1/8" (3 mm).

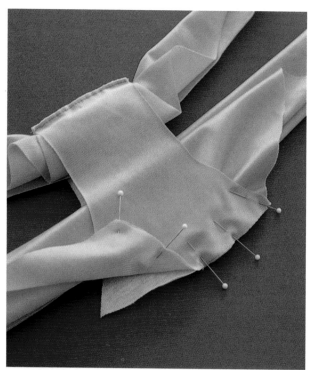

3) Align the crotch piece to pantie back, right sides together, matching centers and ends; pin. To enclose back crotch seam, bring crotch lining under and around panties; pin to wrong side of pantie back, with raw edges even.

4) Stitch seam through all layers of fabric; trim seam allowances close to stitching. Pull out pantie front and back, and turn lined crotch right sides out.

How to Sew Panties Using Flat Construction

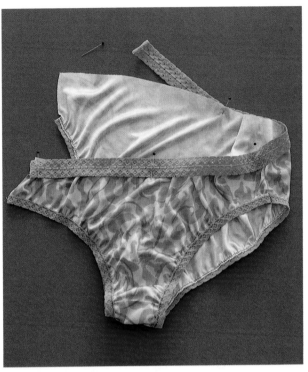

1) Stitch crotch, opposite. Apply elastic to the leg openings, using any method recommended for flat construction (page 54).

2) Stitch one side seam. Apply elastic to upper edge. Stitch remaining side seam.

How to Sew Panties Using In-the-round Construction

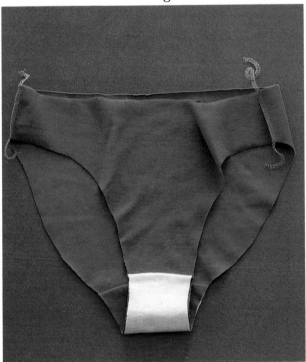

1) Stitch crotch, opposite. Stitch both side seams.

2) Apply elastic to the leg openings, placing elastic seams near side seams. Apply elastic to upper edge.

One-piece Panties

A three-piece pantie pattern can be modified to make one main pattern piece. The crotch lining is also modified. One-piece panties are easier to sew, because the curved crotch seamlines are eliminated. The crotch lining has a straight front seamline. The seam allowance at the crotch back is eliminated entirely, preventing show-through when one-piece panties are worn under pants or shorts.

How to Sew One-piece Panties

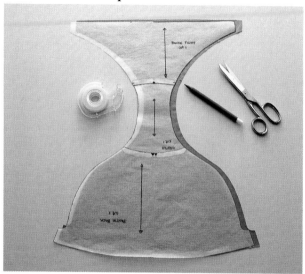

1) **Make** a full-size pattern by tracing the commercial pattern onto tissue paper. Tape or pin the front, back, and crotch pieces together, matching seamlines; cut one pantie from new pattern. Mark placement of front crotch seamline at leg openings of panties.

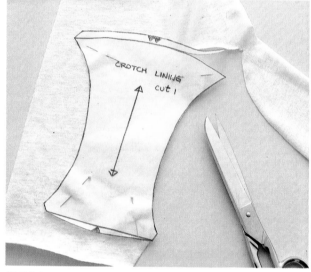

2) **Make** pattern for crotch lining, changing curved front seamline to straight seamline and eliminating seam allowance on back edge. Cut one crotch lining.

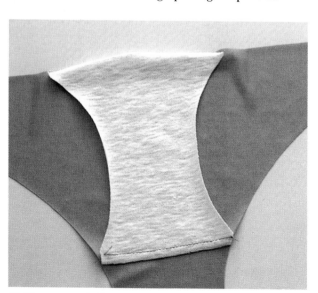

3) **Place** crotch lining right side down on wrong side of panties, matching the front seamline of lining with markings on panties. Stitch seam, using straight stitch.

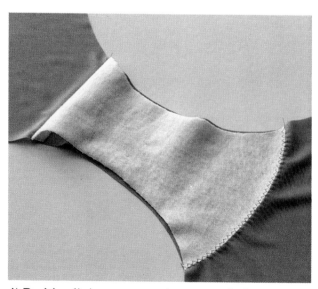

4) **Position** lining over crotch area, enclosing seam. Pin the back edge in place; stitch, using medium zigzag or multistitch zigzag. Complete panties, using flat or in-the-round construction (page 79).

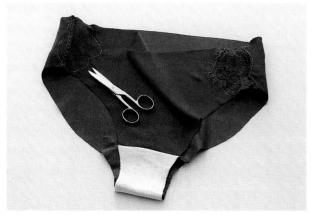

Lace side inserts. Stitch crotch and side seams. Apply galloon lace on pantie front at sides, with scalloped edge of lace ½" (1.3 cm) beyond side seams; use basic method for inserts (page 52). Trim fabric under lace, trimming away side seams.

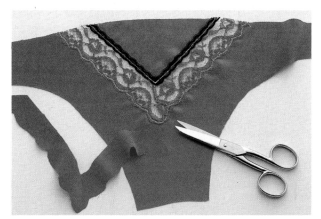

Diagonal lace inserts. Two pieces of lace can be positioned diagonally and overlapped at center front, forming a "V." Trim fabric under lace for sheer effect.

Low-cut front. Measure down 1" to 2" (2.5 to 5 cm) at center front. Mark line from this point to upper edge at each side seam; cut on marked lines. Sew panties, applying stretch lace to upper edge, using overlap method (page 57); lap ends of stretch lace at an angle at center front.

Creative Ideas for Panties

By embellishing panties in various ways, you can have a whole wardrobe of panties, each with a different look. Rosettes, bows, appliqués, and other dainty lingerie trimmings, available at fabric stores, can add just the right finishing touch to the panties you sew. For a low-cut front, change the cutting line at the upper edge.

French Bikinis

French bikinis, sometimes called string bikinis, are constructed differently than traditional pantie styles. French bikinis can be delicate and feminine when sewn in silky fabrics with ruffled "strings" and lace trims. Or they can be durable cotton briefs trimmed with decorative brief elastic or stretch lace.

In the instructions that follow, the reinforced hidden method is used to apply the elastic and the string portion at the side of the bikini is covered with a fabric strip. If desired, the string may be lace-covered instead; using lace ¼" (6 mm) wider than the elastic, cut two pieces of lace the same length as fabric strips, opposite.

When brief elastic or stretch lace is used, the string portion remains uncovered, and the elastic is applied using the overlap method; omit steps 2, 3, 4, and 6, opposite.

How to Sew French Bikinis

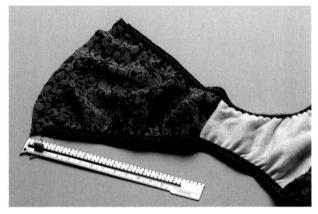

1) Stitch crotch (page 78). Apply lingerie elastic to leg openings, using the reinforced hidden method (page 56), ending elastic ⅜" (1 cm) from upper raw edges of pantie. If stretch lace is used, apply elastic using the overlap method (page 57), ending elastic at upper raw edges.

2) Determine length of side portion of elastic, using elastic guide in pattern. Cut two strips of fabric to cover elastic at sides, twice the length of string plus ½" (1.3 cm); width of strips is twice the width of elastic plus ½" (1.3 cm).

3) Fold fabric strips in half lengthwise, right sides together; stitch scant ¼" (6 mm) seam on long edge. Turn right side out, using small safety pin or loop turner, and press.

4) Overlap ends of fabric strip ¼" (6 mm) on wrong side of pantie front and back, with upper edge of strip down from upper edge of pantie an amount equal to width of elastic. Zigzag ends in place.

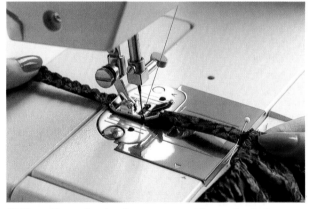

5) Pin elastic to upper edge of pantie, according to pattern placement directions. Apply lingerie elastic to front and back of pantie, as on page 56, step 1, for reinforced hidden method. Or apply brief elastic or stretch lace, using overlap method (page 57).

6) Turn lingerie elastic to wrong side, and stitch, using 3-step zigzag stitch, as on page 56, step 2, for reinforced hidden method; at sides, center the elastic under fabric strip.

More French Bikinis

Once you have learned the basic steps for sewing French bikinis, the possibilities for embellishments are unlimited. The ideas shown here for lace appliqués, lace-trimmed leg openings, and lace pantie fronts can get you started. You can also get inspiring ideas that are easy to duplicate at home from ready-to-wear lingerie in department stores and specialty shops.

How to Sew Lace Appliqués

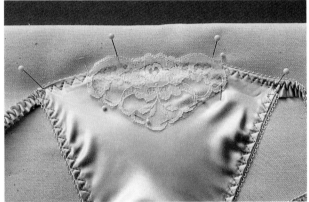

1) Sew basic French bikinis (page 83). Plan appliqué placement at upper edge or leg opening. Stretch the elastic smooth in appliqué area and pin to padded surface. Pin appliqué on right side of pantie, with outer edge of appliqué along elasticized edge. Remove from padded surface.

2) Stitch appliqué on inner edges, using narrow zigzag stitch, backstitching to secure stitches at elastic; do not stitch along outer elasticized edge. Trim fabric and elastic under appliqué for a sheer effect.

How to Sew Lace-trimmed Leg Openings

1) Cut panties from fabric. Trim seam allowances on pantie front leg openings. Tape or pin lace edging or galloon lace on right side of pantie front, with scallops at raw edge of leg openings; ease lace around curve of leg openings, as necessary.

2) Apply lace, using basic, overlay, or reinforced method (pages 43 and 44).

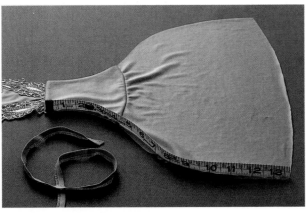

3) Stitch crotch (page 78). Measure leg openings on crotch and pantie back; cut lingerie elastic two-thirds of this measurement.

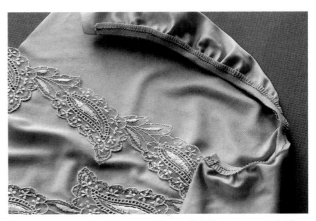

4) Apply elastic to leg openings, folding one end of elastic back at front crotch seam and placing other end ⅜" (1 cm) from upper edge of pantie back. Complete French bikinis as on page 83, steps 2 to 6.

How to Sew French Bikinis with Lace Front

1) Add ¼" (6 mm) seam allowance beyond center front line on pattern piece for pantie front. Cut two front pieces from wide lace, placing scalloped edge of lace at seamline of leg opening.

2) Seam pieces together. Press seam open; edgestitch on both sides of seam. Complete panties as in steps 3 and 4, above.

Tap Pants

Tap pants are versatile and easy to sew. They can be paired with a pretty camisole or worn as an alternative to panties. Different looks can be created by trimming them with either picot edge finishes or bound edges, or by embellishing them lavishly with laces, ribbons, and trims.

Several pattern styles are available, including those with straight legs and high-cut legs. Some are slim-fitting, while others have fullness at the waistline.

Side slits are included in some patterns, but if they are not, they can easily be added to any straight-leg tap pants, using the instructions for mitered slits (pages 64 and 65). For a different look, embellish the side slits with a galloon lace. Or adjust the pattern to make tulip-style tap pants.

Choose a pattern for tap pants based on your hip measurement. To ensure the correct fit in the crotch, adjust the pattern as for teddies (page 93).

The construction of tap pants usually differs from that of panties; most tap pants have inseams and crotch seams, but no separate crotch piece.

Tap Pants with Side Seam Slits

For a pretty finish, add side seam slits to tap pants and use a galloon lace that can be cut in half lengthwise, following motifs (page 16). If the pattern already includes slits, adjust the length of the slit opening as necessary to equal the length of one complete lace motif. After sewing the side seams, apply the lace to the legs, using flat construction. When a wide lace is used, it can be trimmed to a narrower width at the inner legs, shaping the lace

along the motifs or cutting it next to the scalloped edge. This makes a more comfortable and durable leg opening and is necessary when the inseam of the pattern is shorter than the width of the lace.

You will need a length of galloon lace equal to the distance around one leg opening plus four extra motifs. Because the lace will be cut in half lengthwise, this will be enough lace for both leg openings.

How to Sew Tap Pants with Side Seam Slits

1) Stitch side seams. Cut galloon lace in half lengthwise (page 16); position lace on one side of slit, with right sides up and ends of motif at top of slit and at lower edge. Tape or pin in place. Repeat on other side of slit, using remaining half of lace.

2) Clip lace between motifs at corners, to, but not through, outer edge. Position lace along leg opening, overlapping corner motifs. Tape or pin in place.

3) Trim upper edge of wide lace near inseam, shaping lace along motifs or cutting along scallops. Tape or pin in place around leg opening.

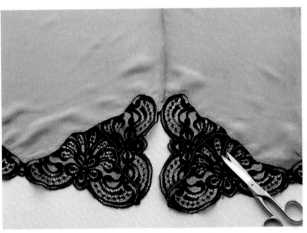

4) Position remaining lace around other leg opening. Complete lace application, using basic, overlay, or reinforced method (pages 43 and 44).

5) Stitch bar tack at top of slit, using closely spaced zigzag stitches.

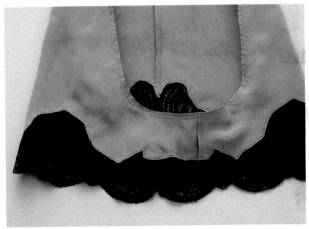

6) Stitch inseams, using flat construction; stitch crotch seam. Apply elastic at waistline, using in-the-round construction (pages 56 to 58).

Tulip-style Tap Pants

Tulip-style tap pants are quick to sew and comfortable to wear. A standard straight-leg pattern is used as the basis for making these tap pants. To keep the original pattern, trace it onto tissue paper before making any pattern changes.

To adjust the pattern for the tulip leg openings, eliminate the side seamlines and extend the pattern pieces at the sides. Sew the tap pants by overlapping the front and back pieces before applying the elastic to the waistline.

How to Adjust a Pattern to Make Tulip-style Tap Pants

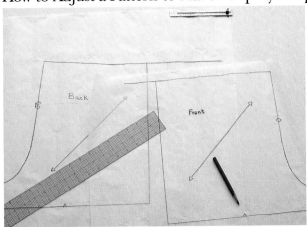

1) Trace pattern pieces for straight-leg tap pants onto tissue paper. Extend waistline of pattern front 3" (7.5 cm) beyond side seamline; extend waistline of pattern back 7" (18 cm) beyond side seamline. Mark midpoints of lower edges.

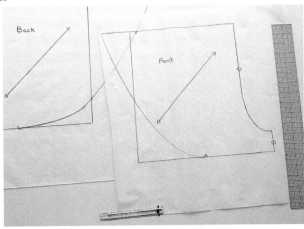

2) Draw smooth, curved cutting lines on both pattern pieces from marking at the waistline to marking at the lower edge. Mark original side seamlines with notches at waistline.

How to Sew Tulip-style Tap Pants

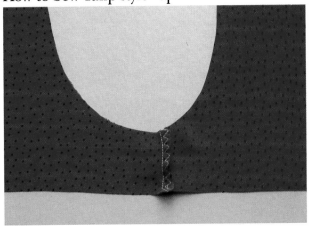

1) Stitch front garment sections to back garment sections at inseams, right sides together.

2) Finish edges of leg openings by applying a narrow lace edging (pages 40 to 44) or by using an edge finish (pages 28 to 35).

3) Lap back of tap pants over front, matching notches at waistline. Machine-baste along waistline edge.

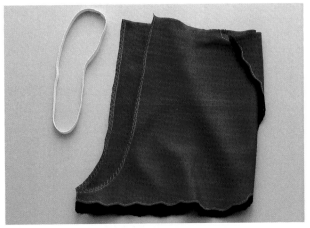

4) Stitch crotch seam. Apply elastic at waistline, using in-the-round construction (pages 56 to 58).

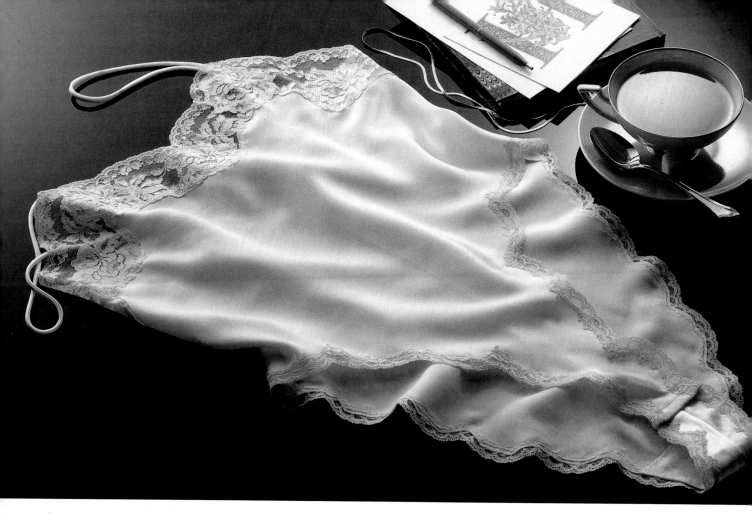

Teddies

A teddy combines tap pants and camisole in one garment. Teddies can be sleek and simple for daywear, or lavishly embellished with ribbons, laces, and other trimmings for romantic loungewear.

Choose a pattern based on your bust measurement, as for full slips and camisoles (page 69), and make any necessary back waist length and full bust adjustments (pages 70 and 71). If you require one pattern size at the hipline and another at the bustline, you may want to select a multisize pattern.

Also adjust the length of the teddy to fit your crotch length, if necessary. A teddy that is too short will pull and bind; one that is too long will add unnecessary bulk under your clothing. If your pattern has a seam at the waistline, you may want to increase the seam allowance to 1" (2.5 cm), to allow for final adjustments during construction.

Choose soft, drapable fabrics such as charmeuse or tricot for sewing teddies. For knits, cut the pattern pieces on the lengthwise grain so the greatest amount of stretch goes around the body; for wovens, cut the pattern pieces on the bias.

The position of the crotch seams in a teddy can affect wearing comfort. Many teddy patterns have four seams that meet at the center of the crotch area. You may want to change the pattern and make a separate crotch piece, to prevent unnecessary bulk in this area. Teddies usually have a crotch opening for convenience. If your pattern does not include a crotch opening, you may want to add one to the front crotch seam (page 95).

Many teddies are seamed at the waistline. For an elasticized seam, use either transparent elastic or baby elastic, cut 4" to 6" (10 to 15 cm) smaller than your waist measurement. The elastic is applied to the seam allowances of the waistline seam, using in-the-round construction, after the bodice and pantie sections are stitched together.

How to Adjust the Length of a Teddy

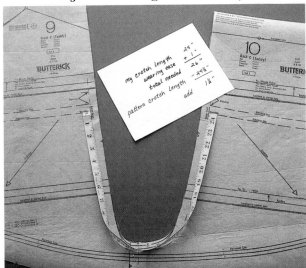

1) Adjust back waist length, if necessary (page 69). Pin pattern pieces together at crotch; measure seamline of crotch seam, from waistline to waistline, standing tape measure on its side. Add wearing ease to crotch length measurement of body (page 13); add ½" (1.3 cm) for very stretchy knits, 1" (2.5 cm) for knits with moderate stretch or bias-cut wovens, or 1½" (3.8 cm) for wovens cut on the straight of grain. Compare the pattern measurement to your crotch length measurement plus ease.

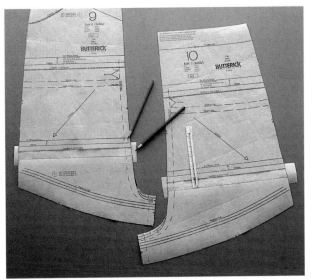

2) Spread front and back pattern pieces on pattern adjustment line, an amount equal to one-half the difference between measurements, if crotch length plus ease is longer than pattern measurement; tape pattern in place, adding tissue paper. If crotch length plus ease is shorter than the pattern measurement, lap the pattern pieces an amount equal to one-half the difference between measurements; tape in place. Draw new cutting lines and seamlines.

How to Sew an Elasticized Waistline Seam

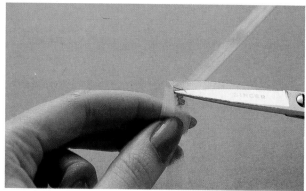

1) Overlap ends of transparent or baby elastic ½"
(1.3 cm); tape in place. Position lengthwise under
presser foot. Starting at center of overlap, zigzag back
and forth, stitching for about ¼" (6 mm). Trim excess
ends of elastic to reduce bulk. Remove tape.

2) Divide elastic and garment opening into fourths;
pin-mark. Place elastic on seam allowances, next to
seamline, matching markings; pin. Zigzag elastic to
seam allowances, stretching elastic to fit fabric. Steam
elastic back to original shape, if necessary; do not
touch elastic with iron.

How to Cut a Teddy with a Separate Crotch Piece

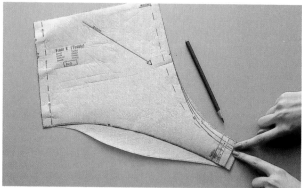

1) Pin the front and back pattern pieces together,
matching inseam and side seam. If pattern has a
crotch closure, eliminate overlap allowance. Crease
pattern at center of crotch; mark the crease as center
placement line.

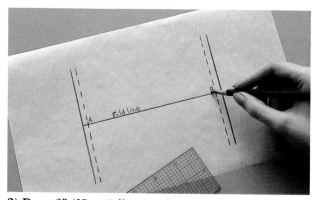

2) Draw 6" (15 cm) line on tissue paper for foldline.
Draw cutting lines at ends, perpendicular to foldline;
draw seamlines ¼" (6 mm) inside cutting lines. Label
Point A for center front and Point B for center back
where seamlines meet foldline.

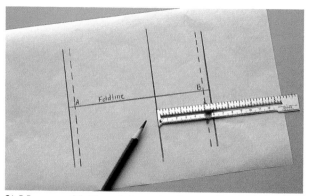

3) Measure 2" (5 cm) from back seamline of crotch
piece; mark center placement line.

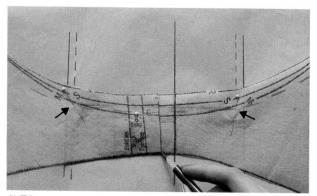

4) Place pattern pieces, pinned at inseam, over tissue
for crotch piece. Pin together, matching the center
placement lines and aligning Point A and Point B to
seamline on pattern front and pattern back (arrows);
foldline will not match seamline. Trace leg opening
from pattern onto tissue to complete crotch pattern.

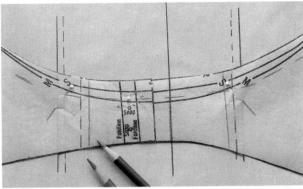

5) Trace back seamline of crotch piece onto pattern back. Draw seamline on pattern front ½" (1.3 cm) from front seamline of crotch piece, toward crotch. Draw new cutting lines on pattern front and pattern back pieces, ¼" (6 mm) from the marked seamlines toward crotch.

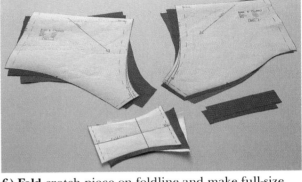

6) Fold crotch piece on foldline and make full-size pattern. Cut pattern front and pattern back on new cutting lines; cut from fabric. Cut two crotch pieces, using pattern; one piece may be cut from cotton single knit. For crotch opening, below, cut two 6" by 1½" (15 by 3.8 cm) bias strips for facing.

How to Sew a Snap Crotch Closure in a Teddy

1) Stitch center back and center front seams of teddy. Stitch crotch pieces to teddy back, in ¼" (6 mm) seam, as for front crotch seam, page 78, steps 1 and 2.

2) Finish leg openings with lace edging (pages 40 to 44), picot edge finish (pages 30 and 31), or edgestitched finish (page 32). For lace edging, use narrow trim on crotch piece.

3) Fold 6" by 1½" (15 by 3.8 cm) facing pieces in half lengthwise, wrong sides together; press. Pin one facing to right side of teddy front, with raw edges even; trim ends ¼" (6 mm) beyond edges of leg openings. Stitch ¼" (6 mm) seam. Press facing away from teddy front, with seam allowances toward facing.

4) Fold facing to inside, folding in ends; press and pin. Edgestitch around facing through all layers. Apply other facing piece to crotch piece, stitching through both layers. Handstitch three snaps at opening, positioning snaps so teddy front overlaps crotch piece ½" (1.3 cm).

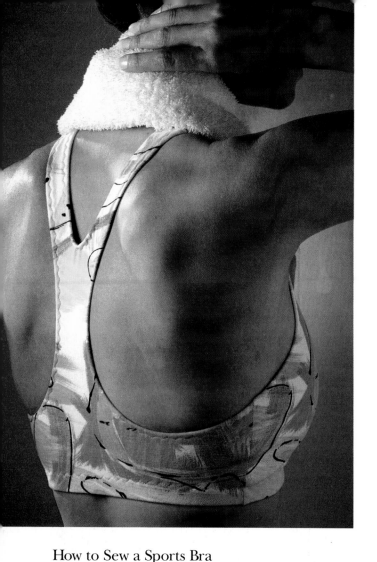

Sports Bras

Sports bras should fit snugly, to restrict movement in the bust area during vigorous activity. Be sure to use a pattern designed as a sports bra. Although swimsuit and other patterns may look similar, they will not provide the proper fit or the necessary support for exercising and sports.

Select a pattern based on your full bust measurement (page 13). When the pattern pieces are pinned together, they should measure 7" to 10" (18 to 25.5 cm) smaller than your full bust measurement. Measure around your rib cage before cutting the elastic for the lower edge; use ¾" (2 cm) braided elastic, cut 4" to 6" (10 to 15 cm) smaller than your rib cage measurement, for greatest comfort. For neckline and armhole edges, use ¼" (6 mm) braided elastic, cut the same size as the garment openings.

Choose fabrics that have 75 percent stretch. Two layers are recommended for firm support; cotton/spandex is the best choice for the lining layer. Cotton/spandex is also appropriate for the outer layer, or choose swimwear fabric or stretch lace yardage.

Try on the sports bra after applying the elastic at the neckline and armholes, and mark the position for the lower edge. Then trim the fabric below the marked line to ⅞" (2.2 cm).

How to Sew a Sports Bra

1) Stitch front lining to back lining at shoulder and side seams, right sides together. Repeat for outer layer of fabric.

2) Machine-baste lining to outer layer, wrong sides together, using a long zigzag stitch; turn the seam allowances in opposite directions to reduce bulk at seamlines.

3) Apply elastic at neckline and armholes as in step 1 for covered method on page 58. Fold elastic to wrong side of garment. Stitch again as in step 3 for covered method on page 58. Repeat for lower edge.

Leggings

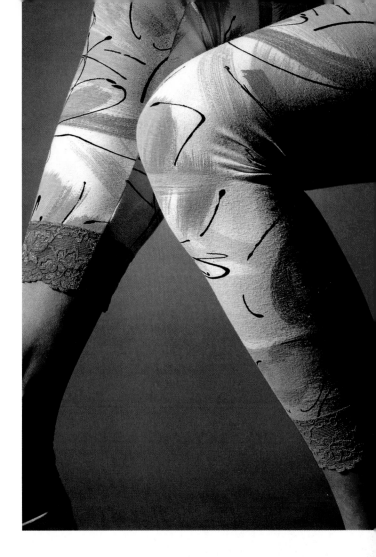

Leggings are close-fitting, yet comfortable. Worn as long underwear, they give the added warmth necessary for cold-weather activities. For a fashion look, they can peek out from under a flouncy skirt or be worn instead of pants under an oversized T-shirt or sweatshirt.

Choose two-way stretch knits, such as cotton/spandex and nylon/spandex, available in solid colors and prints. In addition to plain-knit fabrics, stretch lace yardage may also be used.

Choose a pattern based on your hip measurement; adjust the crotch length, if necessary, as for teddies (page 93).

Finish the waistline using stretch lace, regular, brief, or lingerie elastic, depending upon the fabric and style of your leggings. Use the techniques on pages 56 to 59 to apply the elastic.

Finish the leg openings using a picot (pages 30 and 31) or bound (pages 33 to 35) edge finish. Or use the techniques below for finishing the leg openings with stretch lace, matching or contrasting ribbing, or twin-needle stitching.

Three Ways to Finish Leg Openings

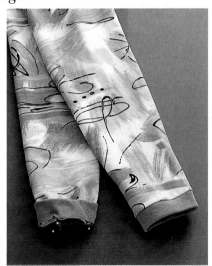

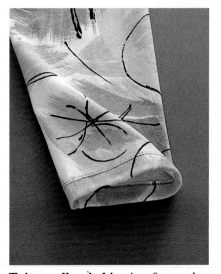

Galloon stretch lace adds a scalloped edge at the leg openings; some laces may be cut in half lengthwise, if desired (page 16). Apply stretch lace using the basic or overlay method (pages 43 and 44); it is not necessary to stretch fabric or lace during stitching.

Ribbing is soft and functional. Cut ribbing twice the desired finished width plus ½" (1.3 cm) by length of leg opening minus ½" (1.3 cm). Join ends in ¼" (6 mm) seam; fold in half lengthwise, wrong sides together. Stitch to leg opening, right sides together, in ¼" (6 mm) seam, stretching to fit.

Twin-needle stitching is a fast and easy edge finish that has built-in stretch for stretch fabrics. Turn seam allowance under at lower edge; stitch from the right side through both layers, using twin needle. Trim the excess fabric close to stitching.

Loungewear
& Sleepwear

How to Make and Apply Gathered Lace with a Heading

1) Cut lace two times the length of finished ruffle. Plan desired width of heading at upper edge of lace; stitch row of gathering stitches this distance from edge, using 8 stitches per inch (2.5 cm). Pull up gathers to fit.

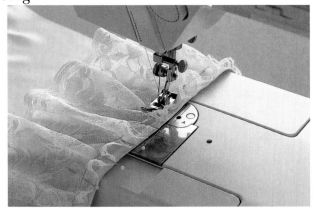

2) Position lace on garment with right sides up; pin in place. Stitch next to previous stitches. Remove gathering threads.

Nightgowns

You may prefer either the elegance of a lacy ruffled gown or the more casual look of a short batiste nightie. The basic fit and construction of either style is usually similar to sewing full slips.

For nightgowns with lace ruffles, pregathered lace trims are available, but for more fullness, you can make your own ruffles by gathering flat lace trims. For a ruffle with a heading, flat galloon lace can be gathered and then topstitched in place on the gown.

On an elegant gown with gathers, plan the placement of a flat lace so the scalloped lace edge is along a gathered seamline. For accuracy, mark the seamline next to the scallops, using basting stitches. Lap the scalloped edge of the lace over the gathered edge of the garment, and stitch along the basted seamline.

How to Apply Flat Lace Using a Lapped Seam

1) Stitch two rows of gathering stitches on edge to be gathered, with one row ⅜" (1 cm) from raw edge and one row at seamline. Pull up gathers to fit, according to pattern. Lap scallops of lace over gathered edge; match basted seamline on lace, above, to seamline of gathered garment section. Pin in place.

2) Zigzag along basted seamline. Trim seam allowance from wrong side, trimming knit fabric close to stitches or woven fabric ⅛" (3 mm) away from stitches.

Sleep Sets

For a flattering,
feminine alternative to
nighties or pajamas, sew a
two-piece sleep set. In this set, the tap
pants and coordinating sleep bra feature a
wide stretch lace band for a soft, comfortable fit.
Use a basic tap pants pattern with high-cut leg openings
and a straight, uncurved waistline. The stretch lace band is
added to the tap pants without any pattern adjustments. The sleep bra
does not require a pattern.

For the tap pants, you will need the fabric yardage called for in the pattern and a length of stretch lace equal to about three-fourths of your hip measurement. For the sleep bra, you will need a length of stretch lace equal to about three-fourths of your midriff measurement plus 26" (66 cm). Either 4" or 5" (10 or 12.5 cm) stretch lace may be used, depending on the desired width of the bands around the midriff and hips.

The sleep bra can be sewn in three bra cup sizes, depending on the full bust measurement: the small size fits bustlines 28" to 30" (71 to 76 cm), the medium size fits bustlines 32" to 34" (81.5 to 86.5 cm), and the large size fits bustlines 36" to 38" (91.5 to 96.5 cm). For the small size, cut four rectangles of stretch lace for the bra cups, each rectangle measuring 3" × 5" (7.5 × 12.5 cm). Cut four rectangles, each 3½" × 5¾" (9 × 14.5 cm) for the medium size, or 4" × 6½" (10 × 16.3 cm) for the large size. These rectangles are cut along the scalloped edge of the lace, as shown on page 104, step 2.

How to Sew a Sleep Bra

1) Fit stretch lace comfortably around body at midriff; add ½" (1.3 cm), and cut. Stitch ends, right sides together, in ¼" (6 mm) seam; backstitch securely. Divide lace tube into fourths and pin-mark; center back is at seamline.

2) Cut two rectangles from stretch lace for each bra cup, right sides together, according to desired bra size (page 102), with matching scallops on one long edge of each rectangle. Draw smooth, curved line from one end of scalloped edge to midpoint on the opposite side. Cut on marked line.

3) Stitch each pair of rectangles along the curved edge, right sides together, in ¼" (6 mm) seam, using conventionally stitched seam (page 27).

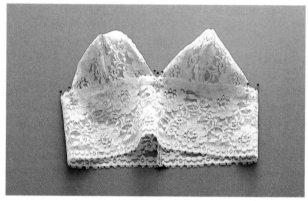

4) Lap upper edge of midriff section ½" (1.3 cm) over lower edge of bra cups; pin in place so scalloped edges of bra cups meet at center pin mark. Pin outer edges of bra cups ½" (1.3 cm) from side pin marks.

5) Stitch along upper edge of midriff section, using narrow zigzag, stretching as necessary to fit. Trim excess fabric, from wrong side, close to stitching.

6) Make straps (pages 72 and 73). Pin straps 4½" to 5" (11.5 to 12.5 cm) apart at upper edge of bra back and at points of bra cups, lapping bra over straps at least ½" (1.3 cm). Try on to check placement and length of straps. Zigzag in place close to upper edge of bra, and again ½" (1.3 cm) away; trim excess straps.

How to Sew Tap Pants with Stretch Lace

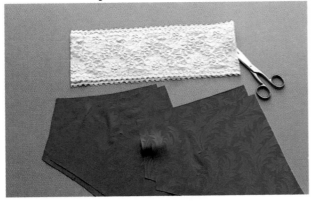

1) Cut tap pants from fabric, eliminating seam allowance at upper edge of pattern. Fit the stretch lace comfortably around body below waistline; add 1" (2.5 cm), and cut. Fold in half crosswise; cut.

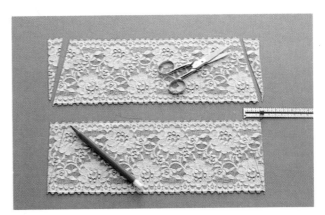

2) Mark 1" (2.5 cm) in from ends of each stretch lace piece at upper edge if using 4" (10 cm) stretch lace. Mark 1½" (3.8 cm) in from ends if using 5" (12.5 cm) stretch lace. Draw lines from these points to lower corners. Cut on marked lines.

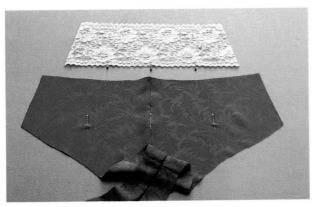

3) Stitch pantie front pieces to pantie back pieces at inseams; stitch crotch seam. Divide stretch lace pieces into fourths at lower edge; pin-mark. Divide front and back of tap pants into fourths; pin-mark, placing pins 4" to 5" (10 to 12.5 cm) from upper edge.

4) Place one piece of stretch lace on front of tap pants, right sides up, aligning the upper edges and matching pin marks; pin in place. Repeat for back of tap pants.

5) Stitch both pieces along lower edge of lace, using narrow zigzag stitch and stretching lace to fit fabric. Trim knit fabric close to stitches from wrong side, or trim woven fabric ⅛" (3 mm) away from stitches.

6) Stitch side seams, backstitching securely at upper edge of stretch lace. Finish leg openings by applying narrow lace (pages 43 to 45) or by using a picot edge finish (pages 30 and 31) or an edgestitched finish (page 32).

Sleep Shirts & Pajamas

Sleep shirts and pajamas should not fit too tightly, in order to prevent binding, straining at the seams, and restricted movement. At the waistline of pajamas, the elastic is covered with fabric (page 58) for a comfortable fit.

Select easy-care fabrics, such as smooth broadcloths and soft interlock knits, that will offer durability and comfort. Fabrics of 100 percent cotton and cotton blends are favored by many. Luxurious silk fabrics are smooth and comfortable to wear, and many silks are machine washable.

Bindings and facings are popular finishes on sleepwear; they may be used separately or together. Both add durability, important for sleepwear that is worn and laundered frequently.

When facings are used, they are often stitched down at the lower edge to prevent shifting. If desired, a facing may be used only at the back neckline, with a more decorative edge finish on the garment front; the shoulder seams are enclosed for neater construction. Back neck facings can be made wider than the pattern for extra durability. When sewn in a contrasting fabric, the wider facing also adds a special detail.

How to Make a Pattern for a Back Neck Facing

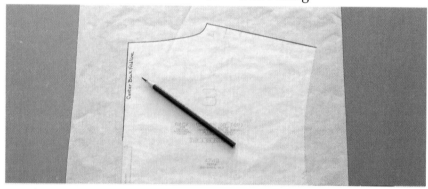

1) Place tissue paper over pattern back. Trace cutting lines of neckline and shoulder; trace center back foldline.

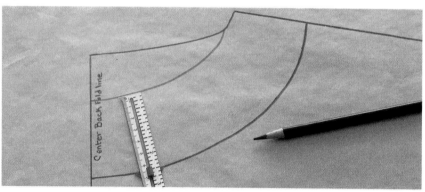

2) Place tissue from step 1 over pattern front, matching center front to center back and matching shoulder seamlines at neck edge; trace cutting line of front neckline onto tissue. Draw cutting line for lower edge of facing, 2½" (6.5 cm) from marking for front neckline. Cut the facing following back neckline and marked line at lower edge.

How to Sew a Back Neck Facing with a Bound Neckline

1) Finish lower edge of back neck facing. Pin or baste facing to garment back, *wrong* sides together.

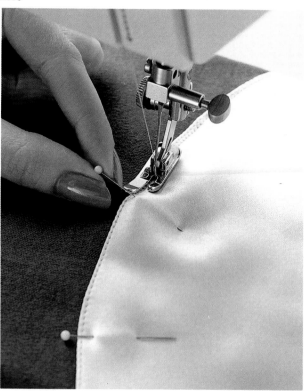

2) Edgestitch lower edge of facing to garment back, if desired.

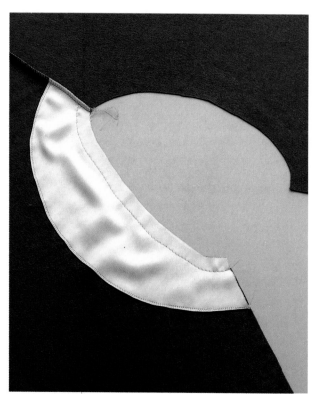

3) Place garment back and garment front right sides together. Stitch only one shoulder seam if using flat construction; stitch both shoulder seams if using in-the-round construction.

4) Finish neckline, using bound edge finish (pages 33 to 35).

How to Sew a Back Neck Facing with Enclosed Shoulder Seams

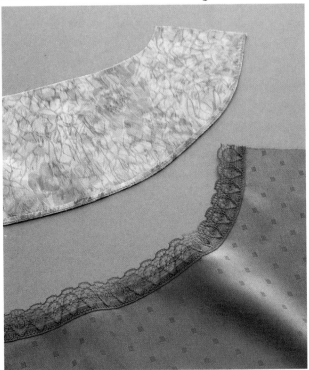

1) **Finish** front neckline by applying lace or by using picot edge finish, bound edge finish, or edgestitched finish (pages 30 to 51). Finish lower edge of back neck facing.

2) **Place** back neck facing and garment back right sides together; stitch neckline seam. Press facing away from garment; trim and clip seam allowances, as necessary.

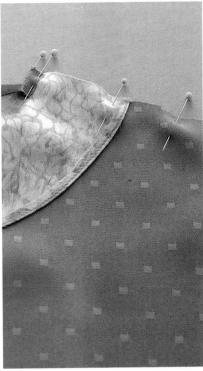

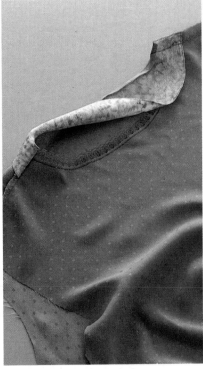

3) **Pin** garment front to garment back at shoulders seams, right sides together, matching necklines carefully. Pin.

4) **Position** back neck facing over wrong side of garment front; fold neckline seam allowances over the facing. Stitch shoulder seams.

5) **Trim** seam allowances. Turn garment right side out; press. If desired, edgestitch lower edge of facing to garment back.

Sleepwear with Fine Piping

Piping adds a tailored detailing to the seams of sleep shirts and pajamas, and may also be used for negligees, robes, and other lingerie. Piping not only emphasizes the design lines, but also makes the seams stronger. Substitute baby yarn, pearl cotton, or pearl rayon for the usual cable cording to achieve a fine, lightweight piping.

For flat piping, the cording can be removed after the piping is applied to the garment. While you are sewing, the cording helps you guide the fabric for perfectly even rows of stitching. The cording is removed from the piping to eliminate bulk; this is especially helpful on lightweight fabrics.

How to Make and Apply Fine Piping

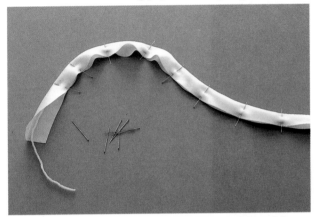

1) Cut a bias fabric strip 1½" (3.8 cm) wide, with length of strip equal to length of seam to be piped plus extra for seam allowances; strips may be pieced together, as necessary. Center baby yarn, pearl cotton, or pearl rayon on wrong side of bias strip. Fold strip over cording, matching raw edges.

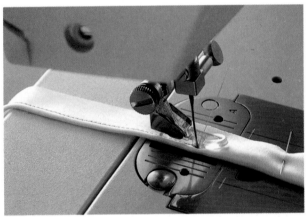

2) Stitch close to cording, using zipper foot. Trim the seam allowances of piping to match the seam allowance of garment.

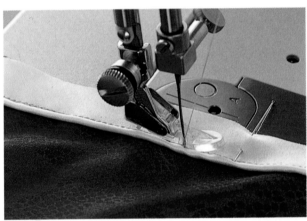

3) Pin piping to right side of garment section, matching raw edges. Stitch, using zipper foot, over previous stitching.

4) Taper ends of piping into seam allowance if using in-the-round construction. At ends of seam, pull out cording slightly and clip it the width of the seam allowance, unless making flat piping.

5) Pin adjoining garment section over piping, right sides together. Stitch seam over previous stitches; for flat piping, take care not to catch cording in stitches.

Flat piping. 6) Pull cording from piping.

Boxer Shorts

Boxer shorts can be sewn in charmeuse to make a luxurious, comfortable garment for lounging and sleeping. Or make a pair from fine cotton broadcloth. Whatever your fabric choice, boxer shorts are quick and easy to sew.

For a comfortable waistband, apply elastic using the covered method (page 58). Be sure to adjust the cutting line at the upper edge of the pattern before cutting the fabric, allowing twice the width of the elastic above the waistline.

Constructing a fly front does not have to be complicated. Whether you use a pattern that includes a fly front or one with a center front seam, you can substitute or add a fly opening that is both simple to sew and comfortable to wear.

How to Adjust a Pattern for a Simple Fly Front

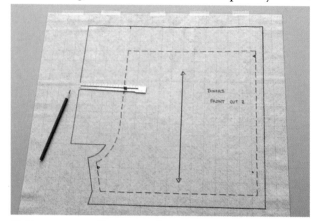

1) Trace pattern front onto tissue paper. Extend pattern 4" (10 cm) from center front seamline, beginning at upper edge and ending 9" (23 cm) below waistline.

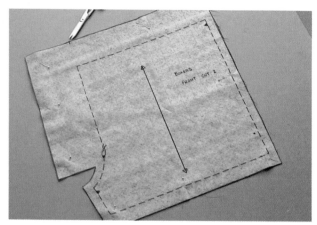

2) Mark dot on center front seamline, ½" (1.3 cm) above lower edge of fly extension. Cut pattern from fabric. Transfer pattern markings; clip-mark center front at upper edge.

How to Sew a Simple Fly Front

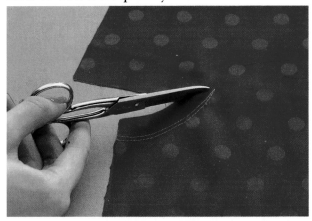

1) Stitch fronts, right sides together, from crotch point to dot; stitch again ⅛" (3 mm) from seamline, within seam allowance, tapering stitches to dot. Clip diagonally to dot.

2) Press under raw edge ¼" (6 mm) on right front extension. Match folded edge to center front; press. Edgestitch from upper edge to dot.

3) Fold left front extension at center front from clip to dot; press crease. Fold under raw edge to pressed crease; press. Edgestitch from upper edge for a distance ½" (1.3 cm) less than fly opening. Pivot and stitch to dot; backstitch.

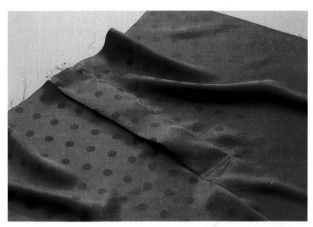

4) Lap left fly over right extension, matching clips; pin. From pivot point, stitch a rectangle, measuring ¼" (6 mm) by width of fly, stitching through all layers.

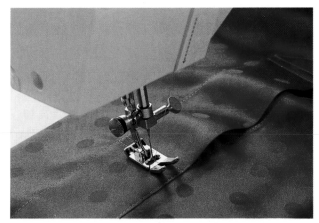

5) Edgestitch from upper edge, stopping 5" (12.5 cm) from rectangle; stitch another rectangle of same size, stitching through all layers.

6) Construct garment according to pattern. Apply elastic at waistline, using covered method (page 58); if desired, multiple rows of straight stitching may be used in step 3 on page 58.

Robes

Robes may be made
from broadcloth or
charmeuse for a lightweight
cover-up, or from terry for greater absorbency
and warmth after a bath or shower. Or combine
two fabrics for a lined robe, selecting a lightweight terry for
the lining. Then make a reversible tie belt (page 119), using
the same two fabrics.

A popular design is a robe with a shawl collar. If you want to line
this style with a terry lining, it is preferable to use a pattern that
has the robe front and collar cut in one piece, to prevent a collar
seam on the lapel. If a pattern with a separate collar piece is used,
eliminate the pattern piece for the facing and upper collar, and use
the undercollar pattern piece to cut both the undercollar and upper
collar.

For ½" (1.3 cm) binding at the outer edges of the robe, cut bias fabric strips
3⅜" (8.5 cm) wide. The combined length of the strips should equal the
distance around the front edges, collar, and lower sleeve edges. Allow extra
length for seam allowances and finishing the ends; piece the strips, as necessary.

You can also line collarless robes that have bands at the front and neck edges
(pages 116 to 119). The instructions, opposite, may be used for lining this robe
style, except omit the instructions for applying the undercollar and binding. The bands on
the robe are applied following the pattern instructions.

How to Sew a Lined Robe with a Shawl Collar

1) **Cut** fronts, back, and sleeves from outer fabric and terry lining; if pattern has an undercollar piece, cut from outer fabric and terry. Cut pockets from outer fabric only. Cut binding strips, opposite. Cut reversible tie belt (page 119), if desired.

2) **Assemble** pieces from terry lining, as follows. Stitch shoulder seams. Stitch center back seam of collar; stitch collar to garment at neck edge, inserting loop into seam for hanging robe, if desired (page 119). Attach sleeves. Stitch side and sleeve seams.

3) **Assemble** pieces from outer fabric, as for terry in step 2, except omit loop at center back and stitch side and sleeve seams, starting and ending with ⅝" (1.5 cm) seam allowance at lower edges and tapering seam allowances to ⅜" (1 cm) in underarm area.

4) **Hem** lower edges of garment, hemming the terry 1" (2.5 cm) shorter than the outer fabric.

5) **Pin** outer garment and lining, wrong sides together, at front edges, collar, and lower edges of sleeves. Trim away seam allowances at front edges and collar; trim seam or hem allowances at lower edges of sleeves.

6) **Machine-baste** along pinned edges. Apply binding as on pages 33 to 35, except stitch binding ½" (1.3 cm) from edge, and for in-the-round construction of sleeves, cut length of binding strip equal to lower edges plus 4" (10 cm) for each sleeve.

Robes with Contrasting Bands

Several patterns are available for the popular-style robe with a band at the front and neck edges. For additional detailing, piping may be added at the seamline when the band is applied.

To complete the look, make a reversible tie belt (page 119) and sew shaped, contrasting bands on the sleeves and pockets. If lightweight fabrics are used, it may be necessary to interface the bands.

Two features can be added to a robe, even if they are not included in the pattern. For attached ties at the waistline, stitch one tie at a side seam and another at the opposite front edge. For convenience, stitch a loop inside the back neckline for hanging the robe on a hook.

How to Make Patterns for Shaped Bands on Sleeves and Pockets

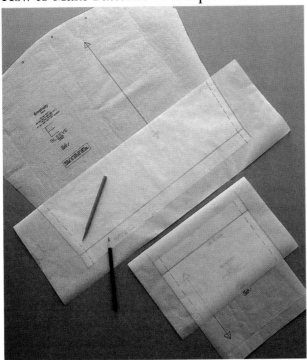

1) Place tissue paper over sleeve and pocket patterns. Mark seamlines and cutting lines at sides. Mark the finished length of sleeve and the finished upper edge of pocket.

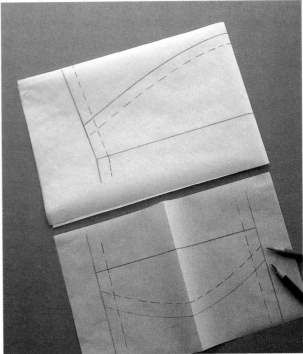

2) Draw seamline for curved edge of band, as desired; fold pattern lengthwise and check that curved line is symmetrical; draw cutting line, adding ⅝" (1.5 cm) seam allowance.

3) Fold tissue on marked line for finished length if sleeve is tapered. Cut on cutting lines at sides of sleeve; unfold.

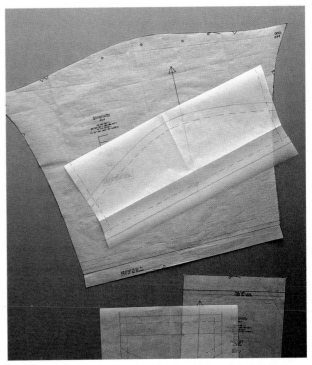

4) Draw new seamline on band, adding 1" (2.5 cm) beyond marked line for finished sleeve length or upper edge of pocket. Add ⅝" (1.5 cm) seam allowances. Draw new seamline on sleeve and pocket patterns, 1" (2.5 cm) shorter than desired finished length; add ⅝" (1.5 cm) seam allowance.

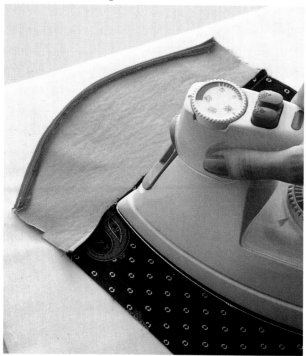

1) **Cut** pocket and band, using patterns (page 117); clip-mark band at upper edge of pocket. Apply piping to curved edge of band, as on page 111, steps 1 to 3. Trim seam allowances; press to wrong side. Place band right side down on wrong side of pocket, matching raw edges; stitch seam. Trim seam allowances; press toward band.

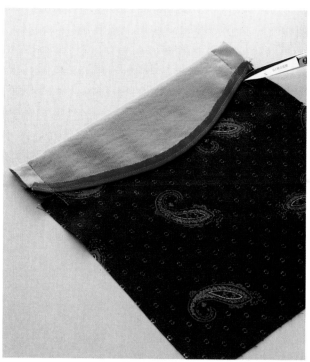

2) **Fold** band at clip marks for upper edge of pocket, with right side of band to wrong side of pocket. Stitch through all layers at sides of pocket; continue stitching ½" (1.3 cm) beyond end of band. Clip seam allowance at end of band.

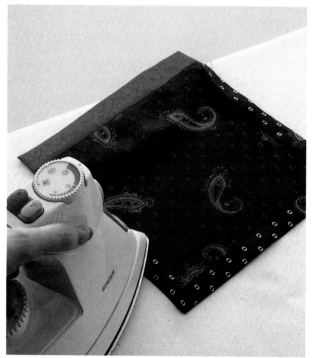

3) **Trim** seam allowances. Turn right side out, folding band down; press. Press remaining pocket seam allowances to wrong side.

4) **Pin** curved edge of band to right side of pocket. Stitch in the ditch or edgestitch close to piping.

How to Sew Shaped Sleeve Bands

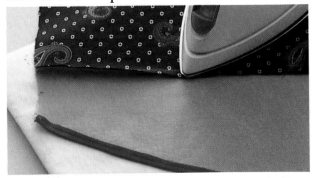

1) Cut sleeves and bands, using patterns (page 117); clip-mark band at finished length of sleeves. Apply piping to curved edge of band, as on page 111, steps 1 to 3. Trim seam allowances; press to wrong side. Place band right side down on wrong side of sleeve, matching raw edges; stitch seam. Trim seam allowances; press toward band.

2) Fold band at clip marks, right sides out; press. Pin curved edge of band to right side of sleeve. Stitch in the ditch or edgestitch close to piping. Stitch sleeve seam if using flat construction; tack seam allowances at lower edge.

How to Sew a Reversible Tie Belt

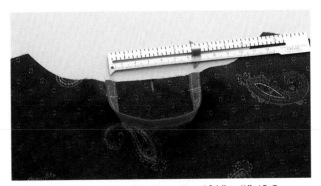

1) Cut two contrasting fabrics, 2½" × 72" (6.5 × 185 cm); if desired, fabrics may be cut on crosswise grain in 36" (91.5 cm) lengths and pieced together. Pin right sides together. Stitch ¼" (6 mm) seam on all sides, leaving a 2" (5 cm) opening at center of one long side.

2) Trim corners diagonally; press seams open. Turn right side out through opening; press. Slipstitch opening closed by hand; or edgestitch on all sides, stitching opening closed at center.

Additional Features for Robes

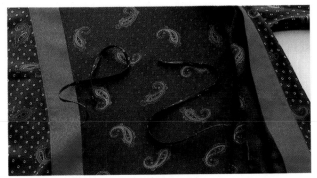

Attached ties. Attach two 15" (38 cm) fabric tubes (page 73) or ribbons at waistline. For women's robe, stitch one tie into right side seam and one at left front edge; on men's robe, stitch into left side seam and at right front edge. Knot free ends of ties.

Back neck loop. Cut fabric strip, 1¼" × 5" (3.2 × 12.5 cm). Fold strip in half lengthwise, wrong sides together; press. Fold raw edges to center and press. Refold, and edgestitch on both long edges. Pin ends 2½" (6.5 cm) apart, centered on back neck edge. Stitch securely into neckline seam.

Kimonos

In Japan, *kimono* refers to a full-length garment that overlaps in the front. Traditionally, kimonos were made from woven panels of silk or wool, 14½" (36.8 cm) wide, that were cut only across the width. Today, the kimono has been embraced by many cultures and adapted to fit modern needs. The kimono is especially suitable for loungewear and is popular for both men and women.

While fabrics are now available in many widths, kimonos are still cut and sewn from one basic shape, the rectangle. This simplicity of form offers an ideal showcase for beautiful fabrics as well as for creative surface design treatments. Kimonos are easy to sew because they are constructed using straight seams. Draft a kimono pattern based on just two body measurements (page 122).

Silk is the fabric most people associate with kimonos. For loungewear, soft silky broadcloth and charmeuse are comfortable and elegant choices. For a more casual look, choose a fine, soft cotton fabric. Cut all pieces on the lengthwise grain, regardless of your fabric choice.

Kimonos are fully lined and have a wide hem.

Traditional kimono sleeves add interesting detailing. On women's kimonos, the lining is revealed at the sleeves.

How to Cut the Garment Sections for a Kimono

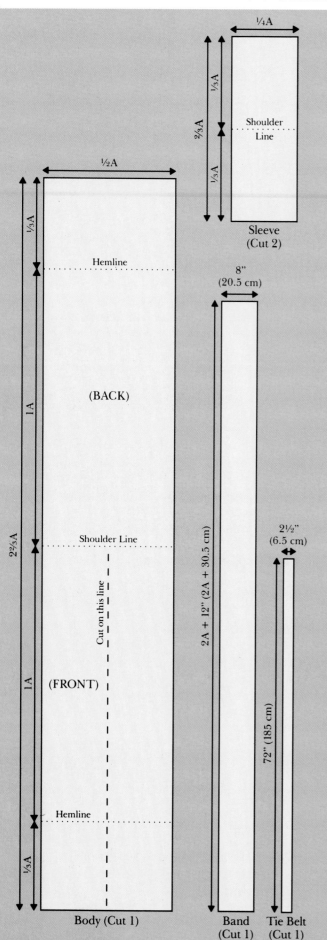

Body (Cut 1)

Band (Cut 1)

Tie Belt (Cut 1)

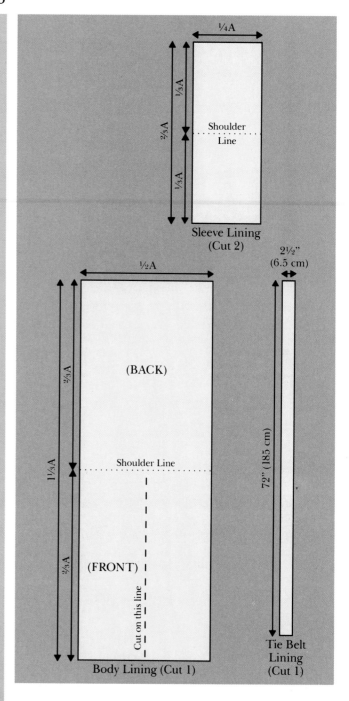

Sleeve Lining (Cut 2)

Body Lining (Cut 1)

Tie Belt Lining (Cut 1)

Measure center back length of body from neckbone to floor; this is Measurement A. Measure around neck to determine Measurement B. Cut garment sections from the outer fabric and lining, based on Measurement A, as indicated, above. For example, width of body piece is one-half of Measurement A, or ½A. Mark notches at shoulder line on sleeve, sleeve lining, body, and body lining pieces. Slash along center front of body and body lining pieces from lower edge to within ½" (1.3 cm) of shoulder line. Measurement B is used in step 8 on page 124 to mark the neckline. Garment sections include ½" (1.3 cm) seam allowances.

How to Sew a Kimono

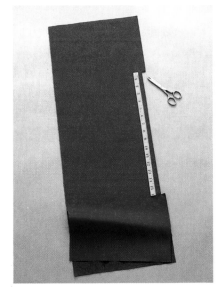

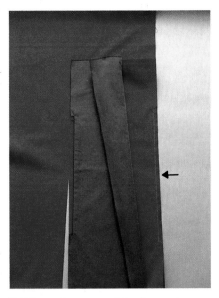

1) Cut garment sections, opposite. Stitch sleeves to sleeve linings, right sides together, beginning and ending 8" (20.5 cm) on either side of notch. Clip seam allowances to stitching at ends of stitching. Turn right sides out; press.

2) Place sleeves and body section, right sides together, matching the notches (arrow) at shoulder lines. Stitch, beginning and ending a distance equal to $\frac{1}{6}$A from notch for women's kimono, or $\frac{1}{4}$A from notch for men's kimono. Press seams open.

3a) Men's kimono. Fold kimono, right sides together, on shoulder line, matching lower edges of sleeve and sleeve lining; pin. Stitch from previous stitching, around sleeve and sleeve lining; end stitching (arrow) a distance equal to $\frac{1}{4}$A from notch at shoulder line of the lining.

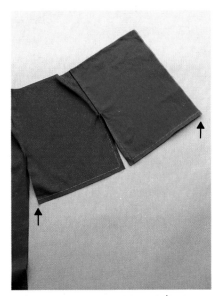

3b) Women's kimono. Fold kimono, right sides together, on shoulder line, matching lower edges of sleeve and sleeve lining; pin. Stitch around sleeve and sleeve lining, starting at lower edge of sleeve and ending at lower edge of lining (arrows).

4) Trim corners. Press the seam allowances open. Turn lining over sleeve, wrong sides together. Press.

5) Stitch side seams of outer garment ending 3" (7.5 cm) from sleeve stitching for women's kimono or ending at stitching for men's kimono. Fold body lining along shoulder line, right sides together; match to shoulder line of outer garment. Mark lining at upper end of side seams. Stitch lining side seams, starting at mark. Press seams open.

(Continued on next page)

6) Stitch lining to kimono at hem, right sides together; press seam open. Fold lining up over outer garment, wrong sides together, pulling sleeves through armholes in lining.

7a) Men's kimono. Reach between lining and outer garment from center front opening; pin and stitch as on page 123, step 2.

7b) Women's kimono. Reach between lining and outer garment from center front opening; pin and stitch as on page 123, step 2 (Seam A). Pin and stitch sleeve to sleeve lining (Seam B). Pin and stitch garment front to front lining (Seam C). Pin and stitch garment back to back lining (Seam D).

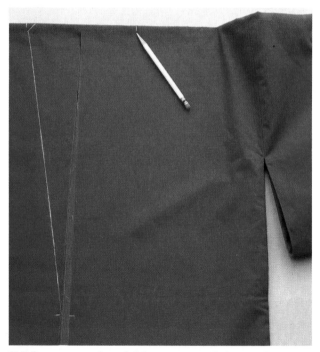

8) Measure one-fourth Measurement B (page 122) on each side of center front along shoulder line; mark lining. Measure 18" (46 cm) down from shoulder line along center front; mark lining. Draw line from center front mark to within ½" (1.3 cm) of shoulder foldline; draw short lines at an angle to fold. Draw back neckline in a straight line along fold.

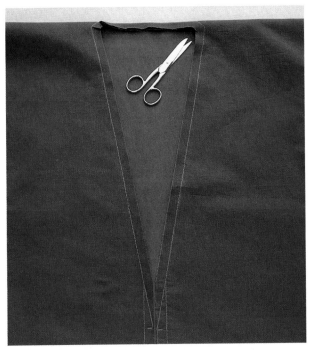

9) Machine-baste ½" (1.3 cm) from raw edges at front opening and along marked lines. Trim fabric ½" (1.3 cm) from stitching. Clip to corners at neckline.

10) Press band in half lengthwise, with wrong sides together and raw edges offset ¼" (6 mm). Fold raw edges in to meet at crease; press. Refold along center line, and press; one side should be ⅛" (3 mm) wider than other side. (Steps shown on three bands for clarity.)

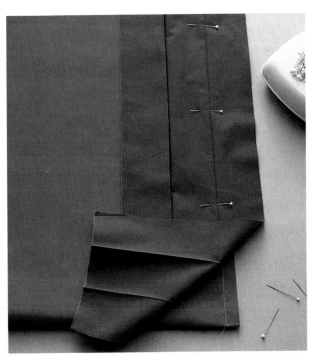

11) Open narrow side of band. Place right side down on lining with fold just beyond basting line and narrow side of band extending over edge of garment; at lower edge, extend band 1" (2.5 cm) beyond hemline of garment. Pin in place; stitch along foldline. Trim other end of band to 1" (2.5 cm).

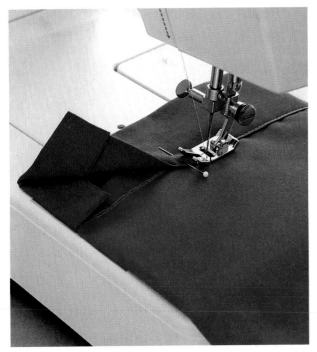

12) Fold band at lower edge even with hem. Fold band around edge of garment; pin. Edgestitch on band from right side. Make reversible tie belt (page 119).

Index

Cy DeCosse Incorporated offers
sewing accessories to subscribers.
For information write:
   Sewing Accessories
   5900 Green Oak Drive
   Minnetonka, MN 55343